GOD'S TALK

Bringing the Gospel to the Isthmus Aztecs of Mexico in their heart language.

To Jim and Nancy,
May God Bless you!
Marilyn + Carl

By Carl & Marilyn Minter Wolgemuth

Copyright © 2011 Marilyn Wolgemuth

All right reserved under International and Pan-American Copyright Conventions. No part of this book may be reproduced or utilized in any form or by any means, electronic or mechanical, including photocopying, recording, or by any information storage and retrieval system, without permission in writing from the Authors.

1st ed.

Library of Congress Control Number: 2011926758

Published by Expertise Inc
100 East 5th St, Suite 300
North Platte, NE 69101
www.IWillAdvance.com

Printed in the United States of America

Design by Candi Bishop

Cover design by Candi Bishop

Summary: For twenty years the Wolgemuths, along with their young daughter Carrie, braved rushing rivers, tropical diseases, insects, and lack of amenities such as electricity, telephones and refrigeration. Those were minor inconveniences compared to the joys of seeing the faces of the Aztec people light up when they discovered they could read and comprehend "God's Talk."

ISBN-10:   1456560824

ISBN-13:   978-1456560829

Dedication

We dedicate this memoir to our dear Wycliffe friends, John and Royce Lind, translators to the Popoluca people, who first welcomed us, worked side by side with us, and supported us as we transitioned into a whole new life, making our home in Mecayapan, Veracruz.

And to the Lind children Cindy, Mike, Laura, Juanita, and Christie who extended friendship to our daughter Carrie.

Thank you!

Marilyn and Carl

Contents

Introduction 3
Summer Institute of Linguistics Study Program 7
Living by Faith: Finances and Prayer 11
Jungle Training Camp 13
Assignment to Worlds Fair: February '64 - July '65..... 23
Back to Mexico 25
Life and Work in Mecayapan, Veracruz, Mexico 29
Language Work 93
Linguistic Analysis and Translation Process 103
Medical Work 137
Religious Practices 151
Beliefs and Customs of the People 159
Rain, Rain, Rain 189
Roads, Bridges and Other Improvements 205
Family Holiday Times 219
Mexico City and Beyond 227
Furlough in the States: July 1970 - September 1971 .. 235
Work at the International Linguistic Center
    in Dallas, Texas 239
A Brief Summary of the Years 1982-1996 279
Acknowledgments 285

Preface

This panoramic account about our adventures in the tropics of Mexico has been gleaned from our extensive journals, diaries and letters written during the years we were members of Wycliffe Bible Translators and the Summer Institute of Linguistics. This book is not presented chronologically. Instead we have reported topics in anecdotal style. Unless otherwise noted, the narrative that follows is written by me, Marilyn.

In this narrative we paint as realistic a picture as possible of missionary life and work. It is tempting to report only the exciting stuff, but we aim to honestly tell it like it was for us. The reader will get a sampling of how our family lived and worked among indigenous people in a remote tropical location and how we made major adjustments to their culture that is so different from our own. We include difficult situations as well as experiences and memories that still bring us great joy and satisfaction.

God's Talk

During this time we struggled to overcome some serious problems that surfaced after we were married and which would hamper us as time went on. (We have written more about this in another book: *The "Ideal" Couple: The Shadow Side of a Marriage.*)

Introduction

Carl grew up in Elizabethtown, Lancaster County, Pennsylvania. His Aunt Anna modeled faithful service by spending many years in Africa as a teacher. He eagerly looked forward to times when she came home and told about her work as a missionary teacher.

I grew up on a farm near Abilene, Dickinson County, Kansas. My parents frequently invited missionaries into our home. Several members of my extended family also served in various mission endeavors. As a child, I loved hearing them tell stories of their work. After my parents retired from the farm, they also modeled sacrificial involvement by generously giving several years to active mission service. So it comes as no surprise that Carl and I both chose the same direction.

Each of our home churches strongly influenced us in the direction of mission work among disadvantaged people. We met at our church-related college, Messiah College, near Harrisburg, Pennsylvania. Carl's interest in Bible translation was first ignited as he read accounts about the profound changes God's

Word had made in the lives of the people-group in southern Mexico who spoke the Tzeltal language. Wycliffe members Marianna Slocum and Florence Gerdel had translated the New Testament into their previously unwritten language. Later I also learned of the many other indigenous people groups around the world with no written language.

How We Heard About Bible Translation

I graduated from nursing school and Carl from college in 1953. We were married in March 1954. The next four years we served as team leaders under the auspices of the Mennonite Central Committee in a Voluntary Service ministry to agricultural migrants in the Coalinga/Huron area of Fresno County, California. It was there in the tiny Baptist church that we heard Wes and Eva Thiessen tell about their transla-

Carl and Marilyn in California during their years working with the migrant workers.

Introduction

tion work with a tribe in Peru. Again our souls stirred within us to consider what our part might be in bringing God's Word to a Bibleless people.

In 1956, the world was shocked by the news that five missionary men were speared to death by the feared Auca tribe in Ecuador. Betty Elliott, widow of Jim Elliott, one of the murdered men, wrote her book, "Through Gates of Splendor" that sparked our interest, even though danger might be involved. Soon after that terrible tragedy, Rachel Saint, sister to Nate Saint (one of the five men), committed her life to live with the Aucas and translate the Scriptures into their language. These were the same people who murdered her brother! (Note: two films were made since 2000, "Beyond Gates of Splendor" and "End of the Spear", that graphically relate the far-reaching life-changing effects that resulted when this murderous group of people believed God's Talk and followed God's Trail.)

When our assignment in California ended, we traveled to Mexico in 1959 to study Spanish. While there we visited Julia Supple, a registered nurse, who was translating the New Testament for the Tojolobal people group in southern Mexico. She also ministered to them through meeting their medical needs. We observed how Bible translation and medical work went hand in hand. Having seen first hand what the medical work was like in a primitive setting, it was very clear to me that my training as a registered nurse would not be adequate in a remote jungle location, far away from medical service such as a clinic or hospital.

On our return from Mexico we rented a cute little house in Los Angeles. We both worked at various jobs, barely scraping together the necessary finances for the next phase of preparation – linguistic training. To better prepare myself medically, I registered for spring semester classes in 1960 at the Bible Institute of Los Angeles' (BIOLA) School of Missionary Medicine, located in downtown Los Angeles. These were intensive courses in tropical medicine, simple dentistry, public health, sanitation and laboratory techniques. I graduated in May.

Marilyn at BIOLA School of Missionary Medicine - 1960.

By the end of the school year, we felt God's call stronger than ever. We began to seriously think about Bible translation work as a meaningful way to follow the Great Commission Christ gave us: to share the Good News of the Gospel with those whose language was still only spoken and had never been written down. They had no way of hearing it in their own language.

Summer Institute of Linguistics Study Program

In June 1960, with our goal now more clearly in focus, we left balmy Southern California to begin this new phase of our adventure in hot, muggy Norman, Oklahoma where we enrolled in the graduate courses that were required before we could apply for membership in Wycliffe Bible Translators (WBT). The Summer Institute of Linguistics (SIL) as a partner with Wycliffe, provided intensive linguistics courses taught by seasoned SIL field members and experienced WBT personnel at the University of Oklahoma. They took time from their own translation programs to prepare novices like us to do the tough job of linguistic analysis and Bible translation anywhere in the world with any language. No specific language was taught, as many people assume; instead the courses were designed to teach the scientific techniques of how to put a spoken language into written form.

Our living quarters were antiquated, rustic army barracks that had been moved on campus from a former army base.

God's Talk

Bunk beds, group bathrooms and <u>no</u> air-conditioning gave it an atmosphere that we were camping out! We didn't know it then but this was excellent preparation for living without the comforts and amenities of civilization in the steamy jungles of the world!

Immediately we were thrust into a grueling pace for ten weeks of linguistic training. It was a similar feeling to being thrown into cold water, sink or swim! The heavy study routine consisted of phonology, phonetics, grammar, cultural adjustment, techniques of learning to analyze and speak <u>unwritten</u> languages, how to form an alphabet and put a language into writing in addition to the basic principles of Bible Translation. How to make primers, dictionaries and grammars of indigenous languages and how to conduct literacy programs were dynamic classes.

September through May we lived with Carl's parents in Pennsylvania. Our daughter Carolyn Joy (Carrie) was born in Hershey. She added a whole wonderful new dimension to our lives! Since she was the first grandchild for both sets of grandparents, they were ambivalent about our plans to take their only granddaughter "to the ends of the earth"!

The following summer it was back to Oklahoma where we faced a second round of advanced linguistic courses that were even more difficult. With a three month old infant to care for, though, intensive study proved to be an even bigger challenge but with adequate child care provided for families, we managed quite well.

Finances were problematic. Our savings didn't reach far enough so our faith was tested to the max. We knew God wanted us there and would supply what we needed. Little did we know that He would frequently provide through

Summer Institute of Linguistics Study Program

our fellow-students and staff. Many times, when funds were especially low, we would find a $5 or $10 bill anonymously tucked in an envelope in our mail box -- enough to buy a week's worth of baby food. There was even a generous gift to pay for a doctor's appointment when Carrie was sick! It was a vivid example of how Wycliffe members care deeply for one another.

Daily chapel services, shared with nearly 300 students and staff, provided rich fellowship and inspiration. We heard many thrilling testimonies of what God was doing for people groups around the world through Scripture translation in their languages that, up to then, were unwritten so the people had no access to God's Word and the Good News of the Gospel. How many of us would be Christians if we had no Bible in our language? We were often reminded of and challenged with the fact that, as English speakers, we have at least fifteen or twenty different versions of the Bible while thousands of languages don't have even ONE version!

Native Americans from several tribes – Kiowa, Arapaho, Cheyenne, Comanche -- were hired as language helpers for the second-year students -- one native American assigned to one student. Carl worked with a Cheyenne person and I worked with a Comanche person. By using the techniques we were learning in the classroom, we were expected to analyze as much of these languages as we could in ten weeks. It took all the courage we could muster for this daunting task. The heavy schedule was exhausting! However, the studies were extremely fascinating and immensely satisfying. Even the hot, humid, rainy weather that make up summers in Oklahoma couldn't deter us from enjoying this challenge, and we successfully completed the program.

God's Talk

We also went through the rigorous application process for becoming members of WBT. What a joyous occasion it was when we got the word that we were accepted as junior members! Becoming full members would come later after further training.

Mose, a Cheyenne Indian holds Carrie on his lap in Norman, Oklahoma.

Living by Faith: Finances and Prayer

Wycliffe Bible Translators is a non-denominational Faith Mission. Each member/couple is responsible for raising financial and prayer support for themselves. There is no fixed monthly salary. Beginning this faith journey was the most daunting part for us -- a journey into the unknown. We heard so many glowing testimonies by our colleagues of how God provided for them and their families so we knew we could trust the Lord to provide our needs, also.

From month to month we never knew how much money would be sent in to Wycliffe headquarters for our support. It was truly amazing how our financial needs were met through generous gifts from churches, friends and family who shared the vision of Bible translation with us. Some contributed regularly and others occasionally. One month would perhaps be lean and the next one fat, but it usually evened out as we economized here and there. Our challenge was to pray and trust God. He always supplied what we needed but maybe not always what we wanted. Sometimes

God's Talk

we had to delay gratification! Nevertheless, believe it or not, one of the thrilling aspects of our life as Wycliffe members was that we never knew exactly how the Lord would provide, but each month he did. Sometimes in surprising ways! In addition to our daily needs, we had enough money to pay our language helpers when they worked with us.

All through our twenty years as members, as we shared the vision and kept our support base informed, our financial needs were taken care of. Wycliffe's policy was not to openly solicit funds, but if people asked us directly what our needs were, we were free to tell them. Otherwise we only shared about how we could see God was working.

Often gifts were designated to cover special needs, e. g. textbooks for Carrie's school work and a yearly enrollment fee in the Wycliffe home-school system. When we spent time in Mexico City on business or for workshops, our expenses were higher than in the language area. Through many loving people the Lord faithfully supplied the necessary funds to keep us in the work He had sent us there to do.

Jungle Training Camp

As Students: February 1962 - May 1962

After summer school ended, we lived with my parents in Kansas for the months of September 1961 through January 1962. They enjoyed getting acquainted with Carrie, their first grandchild. The next step toward becoming full members of WBT was to attend the three-month intensive Jungle Camp Training in Chiapas, Mexico, near the Guatemala border. We were expected to have enough funds on hand to cover the entire three months before we left home. Carl did carpentry work for my uncle David Minter and I worked as a nurse at the local hospital part time. Mother Minter provided child care for Carrie as needed.

We had registered for the first session of Jungle Camp: December 1961-February 1962. Everything was going along rather smoothly and on target when we were suddenly interrupted by my need for emergency surgery in early November. By January 1962 I had recovered sufficiently from surgery so we registered for the third session, February-June.

God's Talk

We had been given a long, long list of army surplus equipment and supplies to buy for this outdoor adventure: jungle hammocks for the three of us, duffel bags, sleeping bags, flashlights, hiking boots, canteens for water on hiking trips, machetes for clearing jungle trails, first-aid kit, and, of course, diapers and clothing. We were limited to what would fit into three army duffel bags – one for each of us. No small task!

To complete the needed amount of money, we had to sell our car. The Lord graciously provided a buyer in a surprising way. Do you get the picture of how we were experiencing this faith journey?

From Abilene, we traveled to Mexico City two days and two nights by train with 11 month-old Carrie. From there we rode the bus another 450 miles to Ixtapa, Chiapas where Missionary Aviation Fellowship was based. The pilots

We are getting ready to take off for Jungle Camp in the Cessna 180 that was specially equipped for the jungle airstrips.

Jungle Training Camp

Main Base at Jungle Camp was a scattering of thatched-roofed houses and tin-walled structures for meeting places.

---

shuttled 40 campers plus 10 children, a few at a time, in the Cessna 180 on a 30 minute flight to the primitive jungle area where the training was to take place. Praise the Lord for Missionary Aviation Fellowship pilots willing to do that! Otherwise, it would have been a hard seven-day hike by foot-trail through dense jungle terrain.

The Jungle Camp training program was carefully designed to prepare new recruits for living under rigorous, rugged conditions without modern conveniences such as telephones, electricity and refrigeration. The program included regular contact with the local Tzeltal Indians as a way for trainees to develop love and understanding of another culture and language. Required reading assignments included missionary biographies to teach us God's faithfulness and perseverance in the midst of problems, disappointments, even persecution.

God's Talk

Those of us who grew up in rural areas had a bit of an advantage over city dwellers! Skills were taught that most urbanites and even country kids know little or nothing about.

We learned how to...

- saddle and ride a horse or burro,
- boil our drinking water,
- gather firewood,
- cook food over an open campfire,
- hang our army-style jungle hammocks from the trees,
- keep our balance on slippery rocks across rushing streams while we carried heavy backpacks,
- slog through pouring rain on trails with mud up to our ankles,
- clear trails through dense jungle growth with a machete,
- swim in swift jungle rivers,
- maneuver a dug-out canoe through river rapids by paddling and/or poling our way,
- butcher chickens, beef and pork, and sometimes wild animals,
- bake bread,
- build a mud stove to cook on,
- wash clothes on rocks in the river and dry diapers over an open fire, and
- provide basic medical care, give injections, first aid and dispense medications for common tropical ailments.

Jungle Training Camp

Survival skills included learning how to:

- use a compass,
- construct a temporary shelter
- make furniture out of bamboo poles,
- send signals to rescuers and identify edible plants and wildlife in case we would ever be stranded or lost for several days.

Weekly mail service came when the MAF plane made a scheduled flight. We learned that we can live without modern conveniences. And we can tolerate and survive the mud, rain, ants, ticks, wet clothes, wet firewood, etc. Sometimes quick tempers and frustrations ran high and patience was difficult to come by! These supposed inconveniences had

Dug-out canoes on the Santa Maria River.

God's Talk

their compensations though, such as God's lovely Creation to enjoy, spiritual oneness and camaraderie with colleagues -- and other blessings that money cannot buy.

As Staff: May 1962 - July 1963

After the training phase was over the end of May, we were invited to serve on Jungle Camp staff. Carl supervised maintenance of the camp facilities and I worked in the camp clinic alongside a local Christian Tzeltal fellow who had learned some basic medical techniques. He was good at caring for the many local people who came for medical care because he could speak their language.

During this time we prayerfully considered which language group God was calling us to live with in order to learn their language and translate Scriptures. We were good friends with Howard and Joan Law who had begun translation work with the Isthmus Aztecs in southern Veracruz who spoke a language called Nahuatl. Due to health problems they could no longer continue there and were hoping another couple would take their place. God placed a desire in our hearts to be their replacement so we stated our preference for this group of people when we were finished with this temporary assignment.

Our family photo taken before we left the US to go to Jungle Camp - 1962.

At that time there were over 140 known distinct indigenous language groups in Mexico who had no written language, including more than one million Nahuatl language speakers. Twelve related Nahuatl dialects scattered over a wide area are still spoken in Mexico, each distinct enough to need separate Bible translations. The Isthmus dialect alone is the heart language of an estimated 45,000 Nahuatl people!

History tells us that Montezuma, the Aztec chief at the time of the conquest, had his armies stationed in various parts of the country. Although Spanish has influenced the vocabulary, the language is still basically what it must have been at the time Cortez conquered Mexico in 1519. It is by no means a dead language.

In July 1963, with our Jungle Camp assignment over, we returned to the States, traveling cross-country from Pennsylvania to southern California, speaking in churches and small groups to share our vision and anticipation of language study and Bible translation in Mexico. At our home church in Elizabethtown, Pennsylvania we were given a special send-off along with their blessings.

In California we got a big surprise when our director asked if we would postpone our tribal assignment and temporarily assume major responsibilities for the Pavilion of Two Thousand Tribes that was being built for Wycliffe at the World's Fair in Flushing Meadows, New York City! There was an urgent need for personnel so we consented to go even though it delayed beginning our work with the Isthmus Aztecs. It was all part of the big picture of Bible Translation. The pavilion was designed to challenge hundreds of others to join with us in the mission fields. We spent the next 18 months on staff at the Fair.

God's Talk

Scouting Trip to Mecayapan - January 1964

Before taking up our duties at the World's Fair, Carl accompanied Herman Aschman, a longtime WBT member on a two-week preliminary trip to the Aztec town where we planned to live. His purpose was mainly to get acquainted with and obtain permission from town officials for us to move there. Mecayapan is 500 miles southeast of Mexico City at the edge of the tropical rainforest in the southernmost tip of Veracruz state.

Carl describes his trip:

The highway to Soteapan is under construction most of the way. Only a truck could possibly go over the deep ruts and huge rocks in some places. The last leg of the trip was on the back of a truck along with soldiers, Indians, baggage, produce, beer and pop. The truck stopped where a fiesta was going on and we were offered delicious tamales for lunch.

It was a gentle climb through semi-tropical oak forest where Popoluca people live in scattered ranchitos *(little ranches) along the way. The driver stopped to deal with coffee growers where he would be picking up bags of coffee on his return trip. Coffee is a big cash crop in this area.*

One of the passengers on the truck was the 2nd lieutenant of the army troop stationed at Soteapan. He showed us splendid hospitality by allowing us to sleep in the armory that night. The next morning two soldiers accompanied us on an hour's trail trip on horseback over hills and streams through jungle vegetation from Soteapan to Mecayapan. Tropical butterflies waved gracefully under sunlit skies. The horses we rode were in no mood to trot so the trip was casual, raising no clouds of dust.

As we rounded a bend in the trail and got our first glimpse of Mecayapan, I wondered: Is this the place where the Lord will permit us to live, love and labor for the next several years? Will we be speaking Nahuatl, knowing these people by name, caring about their ills, their poverty, their ways of thinking, their walk with God? I thought of the years that Howard and Joan Law and their two daughters Susan and Gloria lived here. I prayed "Let it be so, Lord, that we may help bring their work to completion and deliver the precious Word to people we see today."

Herman and I contacted the town authorities, who welcomed us cordially as friends of the Law family. Howard and Joan left a legacy of good will and friendship and for that we were most grateful. The town president gave his permission for me to bring my family to live there when we return next year. During those two days we met many townspeople before hiking back to Soteapan to catch the 2nd class bus to Mexico City. I rejoined my family in the States and we drove on to New York City in the middle of a cold, snowy January.

God's Talk

Assignment to World's Fair
February 1964 - July 1965

In just a brief summary, during our months at the Fair, we served as group housing manager, business manager, pavilion maintenance supervisor, "chief cook and bottle-washer" for other Wycliffe members who rotated shifts at the Two Thousand Tribes pavilion. We entertained many visitors who came to see us and visit the World's Fair. It was a stimulating, rewarding experience to work with so many of the Wycliffe team who came from fields around the world to staff the pavilion. There were tremendous opportunities to share about translation needs among Bibleless people groups with hundreds of Fair attendees! Years later we met WBT members whose first contact with Wycliffe was at the Fair.

Eighteen months later others assumed our responsibilities. This allowed us to return to Mexico and the Aztec people group without further delay. We left with mixed feelings, though, since we had been so involved in the pavilion project, but we knew it was time for us to move on.

God's Talk

Back to Mexico

With our 1955 Buick packed full of our worldly possessions we arrived in Mexico City on August 2, 1965.

Carl describes his feelings about starting village work:

> *As the time came closer to actually go to the Aztecs, doubts and anxiety began to cloud my thinking. The job looked so big and I felt so inadequate in my own strength. Would it be feasible to think of giving village life a try on a trial basis? Fifty percent of my motivation to do this would be to satisfy friends and supporters who know that we have been talking about the Isthmus Aztecs for at least three years. The other fifty percent would be to satisfy my own dream and sense of responsibility.*

In Mexico City we stocked up on enough supplies for up to eight months. We knew we would have to leave our car at the end of the paved road and go in by horseback over the trail so we needed to buy and pack carefully. Our home would be a one-room native-style adobe hut 18' x 24' several

God's Talk

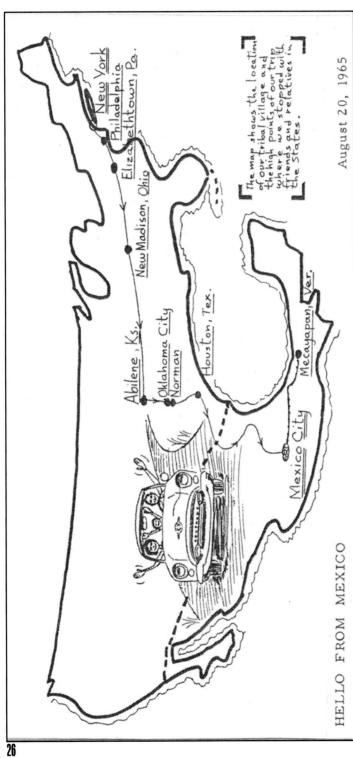

A graphic that Carl drew for us to include in a newsletter we sent back to our supporters detailing the route we took to Mecayapan from Pennsylvania.

miles from the highway.

Now we were ready to be officially allocated, which meant an experienced missionary would be with us for about a month to help us get settled among the people in Mecayapan. Our good friends, John and Royce Lind, translators for the Popoluca people, graciously offered to orient us since their Popoluca village, Ocotal Chico, was only three miles up the mountain from Mecayapan.

This was such a momentous time in our lives. We could only depend on God and His promises to be our strength and wisdom. Four-year old Carrie was too young to know the significance of what we were doing but she learned the language, too, and made friends wherever we went.

Carl was a genius at packing the old 1961 Ford Galaxie we purchased six months later in 1966. He made use of every nook and cranny in the trunk, back seat and the rack he made for the top of the vehicle.

God's Talk

Life and Work in Mecayapan, Veracruz, Mexico

Arrival in the Village - September 11, 1965

On a cool, cloudy morning with our car packed to the hilt and excitement coursing through our very beings, we left Mexico City, passed the two slumbering volcanoes, Popocatepetl and Ixtacihuatl, and headed southeast for Mecayapan. This was a ten-hour drive over narrow two-lane sinuous, mountain roads with steep dropoffs and no guardrails. We arrived, hot and tired, in the tropical Popoluca town of Soteapan about 3:30 p.m. where John Lind and two of his children, Mike and Juanita, met us along with enough of their Popoluca friends to load all our baggage on pack animals.

After greeting everyone, we unpacked the car, piled everything out on the ground to be stuffed into the *costales* (burlap sacks) and tied on the mules. As a way of saying thanks for their help, we bought a bottle of warm Pepsi for everyone,

God's Talk

(no refrigerators in this part of the country!). Señor Adolfo Carmona graciously permitted us to park our car by his store for safekeeping.

Bidding "adios" to Señor Carmona, our motley entourage left Soteapan with Carrie and Juanita riding on one donkey, me on Lind's mule and Carl hiking with the rest of the group. Several Popoluca ladies brought up the rear. One of them balanced my bright red tote bag on her head. Tied to that bag was the shiny red helium-filled balloon that Carrie had gotten the week before at the zoo. It was a rough three mile hike over the hills and muddy trail that took us to the Popoluca village of Ocotal Chico where Linds lived and worked on the language. What a comical, colorful procession we must have made as we trudged up and down hills for nearly two hours, waded across a small stream and larger river and perspired profusely in the tropical heat!

After the last river crossing and a stiff climb up the last hill, we came to the pleasant pine grove on rolling green grassy hillsides. This was the Popoluca village of Ocotal Chico. What a relief to finally arrive and be greeted by Royce Lind who had a delicious supper of beans, rice and tortillas ready for us. Never has simple food tasted so wonderful!

We settled down for the night in their thatched-roof guest hut and were lulled to sleep as we listened intently to the various jungle sounds all around us -- crickets chirping, donkeys braying, dogs yapping, a thunderstorm brewing in the dark sky, voices of next-door neighbors chattering in their staccato Popoluca language, soft raindrops falling on the thatch. In spite of being very tired in these strange surroundings, and apprehensive about what was ahead of us, we slept soundly.

Life and Work in Mecayapan, Veracruz, Mexico

Our Living Environment

After an early breakfast the next morning, John, Carl, Carrie and I hiked down the mountain for one and a half hours to Mecayapan where we planned to live and work among the Aztecs. Royce packed a tasty lunch and drinking water for us. Carrie rode the burro and I rode the mule while Carl and John walked. The burro Carrie was on spied another burro and started chasing it. Carrie hung on for dear life, screaming at the top of her lungs. Three or four minutes later Carl and John caught the burro's bridle. Shaken up but obviously unhurt, she still wanted to ride the rest of the way but only if John led it with a rope!

On our arrival in town, Carl went to get the key to Law's house from Porfirio (Among ourselves we called him "Fred.") He was one of the shopkeepers in town who had kept watch over the house. At first Porfirio didn't recognize Carl because his face was clean-shaven. The year before when Carl visited he had a moustache and left with a four-day beard. Carl, John, Carrie and I walked over to city hall and introduced ourselves to the town officials. What kind of reception would we get? We saw several women and children staring at us from a distance. Would they accept us eventually and become our friends?

As long as we live we will never forget the sight that greeted us when we opened the door of the 20' x 24' adobe house where we expected to live! The few rustic furnishings Laws had left there six years before were covered with dust, rat and bat dirt. Carl counted seven bats hanging from the rafters. At times they flew around but mostly they just hung there by their hind legs. We discovered rat nests in the boxes of kitchen utensils, pots and pans. Carrie was intrigued by the baby rats that she thought were cute enough to play with. Mother had different ideas, however!

John spied a bucket in the corner and took it down the hill to get water at the river. I located a basin and scouring powder to clean off the wooden table and chairs so we could sit down and eat our lunch at noon. We were famished enough to eat in spite of the filth surrounding us. We sat down gingerly and devoured the cheese sandwiches, boiled eggs and beans Royce had fixed for us.

Taking inventory and listing items we needed to buy next time we went to town turned out to be a dirty, unpleasant job. Most kitchen items were still useable if we scrubbed and disinfected them vigorously -- dishes, a few pots and pans, shelves, cupboards. Enough for one day. Now to trudge back up the hill to Ocotal Chico for the night.

After an uneventful hike back over the trail, Royce's hot soup, cornbread and lemon meringue pie tasted like a gourmet meal. The bed felt even better. Every muscle in our bodies ached. By 8:00 p.m. we were sound asleep. We were so thankful for the Lind's gracious hospitality while we prepared the house to live in. I don't even want to imagine what it would have been like had we not had their loving support!

The rest of the clean-up would take several days of hard work. The rough cement floor needed a good scrubbing, and the brown adobe walls could be white-washed. Each of the four adobe walls had a small screenless window with wooden shutters that opened inward. Rats had chewed huge holes in the walls that needed to be re-mudded. The whole south wall would need to be replaced with fresh adobe. Between the tops of the adobe walls and the corrugated tin roof was a twelve-inch space that provided lots of natural

Life and Work in Mecayapan, Veracruz, Mexico

This house is what greeted us as we arrived in Mecayapan.

air-conditioning. One of our first projects would be to close that gap by stretching wire mesh the whole way around the top of the walls to keep the rats and other critters out! There were weeds to cut and a fence to put up to keep out the pigs, turkeys and dogs that wandered freely all over the village cleaning up after the people. Before we left, John and Carl arranged for several village men to help us.

The next two days we scrubbed nearly everything in the house with soap and Clorox water. Carl got the three-burner table-top kerosene stove to work. It rained each day so we scraped lots of mud off the floor. What a sloppy mess! By the time we were finished my poor, sore hands were rough as sandpaper and needed to heal. (Later we added a porch on to the house so the mud wouldn't come right up to the front door.)

The next day four men came to re-build the south wall. The local method of constructing a mud wall was to first make a big puddle of mud that they mix with their feet until it's just the right consistency. They take fistfuls of that mud

God's Talk

and mix it with long-bladed grass, then hang globs of the grass/mud/gumbo over a lattice work of split cane strips and smooth it like plaster. A rough and asymmetrical adobe wall was finished by noon the next day but it was strong and would do the job of protecting us from the elements and critters.

We watched the shy native women as they walked past our house on their way to the river to get drinking water, bathe themselves and their kids, wash clothes by slapping them on the river rocks and rinse their cooked corn for making tortillas. They would giggle, whisper and glance surreptitiously our way. Who knows what they were saying about these strange, paper-white-skinned people! What was it about us that was so fascinating? I greeted, waved and smiled at them, and they waved back. If only I could understand just a quarter of all they are saying! I will someday.

The big moving day. What a spectacular show we must have put on for the Popoluca people in Ocotal Chico as we again lashed everything on pack animals and trudged down the trail. On our arrival at the house, the children were so curious. They hung in the open windows, crowded the doorway, sat on the bench just inside the door, and chattered an endless commentary on our every move. With eagle eyes, they watched our every move from early morning until we gave a gentle (?) hint at night that we were ready to retire. It was like we were monkeys in a zoo or fish in a fishbowl!

One of our last tasks was to get the rough-hewn double bed for Carl and me and a cot for Carrie ready to sleep on. These we covered with four-inch foam mattresses that we bought in the city. We put on the clean bedding that we brought with us then we hung mosquito netting around each one to hopefully keep out any critters. We were ready to crash. By the end of the day my patience was tested severely and I was about at my wits end, but I reminded myself that these were excellent opportunities to learn new vocabulary.

Building the Outhouse and Shower Stall

During our first month, going to the toilet meant walking about 75 yards to the "bushes" nearest our house, just like everyone else in town! No one here had ever seen a pit-toilet so it created quite a flurry of curiosity when we started building one soon after we arrived. We hired three of the local brethren to help us for three days with the project.

The first thing was to dig a pit six feet deep and four feet across. Two men split bamboo cane to make a framework for the walls. Then, after mixing mud and grass with their feet in a hollowed-out space, they skillfully slapped globs of this mixture over the framework and smoothed it out with their hands for a textured plaster appearance. The rich, brown color of the adobe mixture blended into the landscape very appropriately. A platform and seat was then built over the pit. Only the door was lacking, so a curtain served temporarily until we could get to town for the needed supplies. What a relief to have privacy!

The workmen ate noon meals with us. So what did I feed hungry men? Something very simple: black beans or rice with a bit of meat, tortillas, fried bananas and lemonade were good choices. Or goulash, tortillas and banana cake. For dessert one day, I served canned peach halves in heavy syrup. At first they thought they were raw eggs!

A day or two after the toilet was completed, several men came around to chat with Carl. The conversation centered around the outhouse and he offered to show them how it

God's Talk

Both men and boys were involved in the construction of our outhouse. Here the bamboo slats are ready to be covered with mud.

was built. They looked it over very carefully and one fellow tactfully remarked, "Now you've shown us how these things should be done." Other comments weren't so positive, though. Some people thought it was "gross." They preferred to keep using the bushes that have served the community for a very long time.

The river at the bottom of the hill was where we usually went for our daily bath. It was often muddy and uninviting, especially after a rain, which was nearly every day. A year later Carl ingeniously used his creative construction skills to build a closed-in shower stall attached to the side of the outhouse. A slatted, wooden platform to stand on allowed the water to drain out on the ground and kept our feet from getting muddy. To take a hot shower, we first had to heat water on the stove in a metal bucket and then pour it into a five-gallon can on which Carl had welded a shower head and

Life and Work in Mecayapan, Veracruz, Mexico

valve. With a rope on a pulley, we hoisted the can of water onto a shelf above the platform so we could stand under the shower and let the warm water refresh us. On hot days we didn't bother to heat the water. A cool shower in the middle of the day felt good.

Remodeling and Redesigning Our House

One project was to add a porch on to the front entrance, a big improvement over the sticky mud being right at the door. The second project was to put up a fence around the house and a small garden plot to keep the roving pigs, turkeys, chickens and dogs from coming in.

The porch added a whole new dimension to our living and we made good use of it. Carl put a rope swing on the porch for Carrie and all her little friends that came around. It was a good rainy day pastime for them. The porch served as our

Marilyn visits with the ladies on the front porch.

God's Talk

classroom. The young pastor and his wife came to meet us and others came to give us lots of exposure to conversation. As many as 23 people were here at one time to visit, men, women and children.

All this time we were busy getting adjusted, we put in lots of time to learn the language. We wrote words down on 3x5 cards and filed them in a shoebox to be reviewed and analyzed later. We felt blessed that the townspeople were so friendly and willing to help us get the words right! They laughed heartily with huge guffaws as we made multiple attempts to pronounce the phrases. We provided lots of entertainment with our clumsy linguistic efforts.

Carl and his helper, Hipolito, replaced the front door with a new "double dutch" door so we could have just the upper half open if we didn't want people to walk right in. The construction made a lot of dirt and noise, complicated by interruptions with the sick ones who needed treatment. (I decided to call them "opportunities" rather than interruptions, because the people are what we came here for.)

Later we built a medium-size free-standing fireplace in the middle of the living area. It served us beautifully on cool, breezy winter mornings and evenings when the north winds blew in through the space above the walls. On cold days, we kept the fireplace going all day. In the evenings Carrie and I would sit by the crackling fire and read aloud by kerosene lamplight the Narnia series and other favorites. Popcorn was a new thing and our visitors loved it when we shared it with them around the fire.

Our visitors were amused to see that we had a fire in the house like they have! The only difference is that they make fires on the dirt floor in the middle of their hut with the

Our house soon became more comfortable with the porch added along with the other changes we made to it.

---

smoke filling their living space. Ours was built on a pedestal with a metal chimney through the roof to direct the smoke up and out.

As time went on, we added a kitchen, combination study/workshop, space for the medical work, a room for more visitors, a loft bedroom for Carrie and a mouse/cockroach-proof storage room. We added a carport after the big bridge was built and we could drive the car into the village. These additions all had packed earth floors.

The house-remodeling was completed in 1970 when two summer volunteers helped us install a kitchen sink and connect the faucet to the rain barrel outside the kitchen that caught and stored roof water when it rained. During the rainy season June-February, we enjoyed plenty of water in the rain barrel. How wonderful! It sure saved time and effort from carrying water from the river.

God's Talk

A Random Peek into Our Daily Life

Carl writes reflectively:

Temperatures in the mid 50's are as cold as it gets in the tropics. During January and February it is drizzly and cold, hampering our activities. Cold fronts called **nortes** *(northers) move in across the Gulf of Mexico. With our "natural air conditioning" a sweater feels good at night. News from the U. S. is that a deep freeze is in many areas. Marilyn is baking bread, Carrie is taking her semester tests. Lucas isn't here today. Tomorrow he will come again. Yesterday we translated 17 verses in Acts 17.*

Had such a wave of selling popcorn we are all glad that it's gone now. This morning a little girl came to buy paper "that's heavy" for wrapping books. I sell them newspapers that I buy in town.

There are lots of coughs and colds in the village now. Many people have no warm clothing. Even if they did, they would have no good place to store them during the hot months of the year.

I woke up about 6:00 a. m. to the sound of chopping. Maybe Tomas is carving out a trough or something. I didn't get up right away. Had a coughing spell during the night and didn't feel very perky from this cold I have. Our bed is comfortable with a four-inch foam over a rigid plywood platform. Marilyn was up and dressed and the sun was already shining when I got up later.

We had a very light shower yesterday, the first for about two months. March, April and May are the dry season. The weath-

er will gradually change now from dry and cloudless to the more humid but cooler summer with thundershowers almost daily. Yesterday as it was raining we realized that we had almost forgotten the sound of rain on our galvanized roof. It is such a welcome sound even if muddy trails are the outcome!

I walk out the bedroom door that opens directly to the north and wobble over the cobblestone path under the eaves to the mud-walled toilet. The walls of the toilet come to just below my eye level, so as I stand there I can look out toward the north and see the neighbors' grass-roofed huts. The calabash tree is there with its bright green globes swaying in the breeze. Beyond that I see a donkey with only two stubs for ears. There is nothing truncated about his shrill bray, though!

The shower stall is attached to the toilet. I have to stoop a little to get in because of the rain gutter between the two roofs. I notice that the wash basin still contains water from a previous hand-washing. I pour the reddish-brown water outside by the blooming hibiscus bush.

That bush is showing signs of thirst and the flowers have been small lately. I dip two gourd-bowls full of water from the bucket into the basin, carry the basin into the house, through the bedroom into the kitchen, and put it on the gas burner. While the water is heating I pad through the house to the south room, which is my study and workshop. It resembles a closed-in porch, except the walls are split oak rails with wide cracks between.

Next is the bamboo window shutter. I remove the nail that keeps it shut, swing it in and up and hook it in place. Sunlight floods the workshop. I notice the packed-earth floor is in pretty good shape from yesterday's sprinkling. If we don't sprinkle every day it becomes a dust floor. Marilyn keeps it looking good

God's Talk

by lugging around a two gallon sprayer filled with water. To keep it smooth and packed solid we soak it good with buckets of water once every few days before going to bed.

By the time I return to the kitchen the water is hot. I carry it back through the bedroom, across the cobblestones, under the rain gutter and set it down on the shelf under the mirror in the wash room. I look into the mirror. UGH! I need a haircut bad. Shaving done, I walk into the study and my day's work begins. A little lizard just caught my attention as it moved along the dirt floor near my desk. Soon it scampered out between the split oak rails.

I am too often irritated by people. This morning I realized what irritates me, my time is demanded by people for things that to me are secondary and as yet there is so little demand for the materials I am translating. This is the main reason I'm here, and which I want them to want.

The thought came to me recently that these very demands give me an opportunity to do what I can to interest people, if only I will realize it at the time and cheerfully serve the people's needs. But if I don't, my poor attitude will repel people from becoming interested.

Marilyn's journal entries:

When we returned from linguistic workshops, our friends gave us a warm welcome and deluged us with produce from their fields, corn on the cob, black beans, oranges, bananas, papaya, stalks of sweet, juicy sugar cane, hot tamales and freshly laid eggs. One time, a few of the ladies noticed I was about 10 pounds heavier and had a few more gray hairs. They exclaimed in Nahuatl: "My, how big your fatness is and your head is getting ripe!"

Another time, the corn our neighbor planted in our garden plot was ready for eating. The weeds were high outside the fence. The cockroaches had proliferated in the house. The house itself was in good shape but the walls of the outhouse needed to be re-mudded due to some erosion.

Juanita Lind came to live with us for six weeks while her parents were away. She and Carrie had become great friends. One night Juanita's mare and filly were stolen! No clue as to who or how. She was tied right in front of our house, too. Horse thievery was taken very seriously here! Bulletins were put out on the radio and to law enforcement. Five weeks later the town authorities notified us that the mare and filly were found 50 miles away near Acayucan, our market town. When Carl, Carrie and Juanita went to Acayucan to get them, they were told that the young fellow who stole them had already confessed and was put in jail.

Carrie was excited when our little red hen laid her first eggs. Sammy's mother had given us the chick in September. We came back from a day up in the pines one Sunday and, sadly, our little red hen was dead, lying beside her freshly-laid egg. Maybe it was the chlordane insecticide we sprayed around the house.

The three of us spent an unusually warm January day and evening in our pine woods. Made a bed of soft, fragrant pine needles and pretended we were going to sleep there. Carrie wanted so much to sleep there all night, but our village friends and neighbors watch us so closely and often comment on our strange behavior. We didn't think they would understand if we *spent the night in the pine forest. So we wended our way back to our house with a big full moon to light our way.*

About sun-up each day we could count on people to stop by on the way to their fields to ask for medicine or to return something they borrowed. Breakfast time, time to make the daily contact by two-way radio with our Mexico City headquarters 500 miles away. By 8 a.m. the breakfast dishes were done, Carrie took the horse to water and cut grass for him. Then she began her day's home-school studies. Carl began the work he had going at the time. We were "on call" 24/7 for medical consultations, emergencies and dozens of other interruptions. Each one was an excellent opportunity to listen to more language and learn to know the people and their culture better.

A broken machete blade became a shoe-scraper next to the front door. Thankfully, most of the mud stayed outside where it belonged. The new roof gutter worked perfectly for the rainwater to run off the galvanized metal roof into a fifty-gallon barrel under the eave outside at the corner of the house. We used that water for bathing and washing dishes.

Soon after we settled in, our friendly next door neighbor graciously offered to take our laundry to the river and wash it for us. Her daughter, equally helpful, offered to carry our drinking water up the hill from the pozo *(water hole). She balanced a full three-gallon bucket on her head, walked up the rather steep hill and not a drop would spill out! I paid both of them what I thought was a fair wage. We boiled the water for 10 minutes to make it relatively safe to drink, or we used a small amount of diluted iodine solution in a five-gallon container to purify it.*

Without electricity in the evenings we made good use of kerosene lamps. Naturally, we missed the convenience of refrigerator, sink, bathroom, telephone and electric lights. Our valuable

Life and Work in Mecayapan, Veracruz, Mexico

Jungle Camp Training came in to play as we adjusted to this radical change of environment. This was for real!

Examples of what we could be heard saying:

- I must boil drinking water yet tonight.
- Tomorrow is meat day. Carrie, you may grind the meat for hamburgers.
- Shall we smoke some of the meat this week?
- Don't forget radio time (daily two-way contact with MAF and other missionaries in Oaxaca and Mexico City).
- I'll wash the lamp chimneys. Could you fill the kerosene lamps?
- The trail was pretty good today. It hasn't rained for a couple of days.
- I'll mix up some powdered milk and we'll have a bedtime snack.
- Wet down the dirt floor and then I'll sweep it.
- Uncover the rain barrel; it looks like it will rain tonight.
- I've got to look for ticks. I'm itching like crazy!
- Tuck the mosquito netting in good.
- HCJB radio station (in Peru) is coming in good and clear today.
- I wrote down that word yesterday, now let me see, what does it mean?
- We'll soon need to order worm medicine again.

God's Talk

Neighbors and How They Live

Early morning life in the village was never boring. We heard a cacophony of sounds all around us as villagers began to wake up. A raucous rooster chose our yard to crow the loudest about 4:00 a.m. That was the signal for our neighbors to begin stirring around in their huts. A child whimpered. A dog barked urgently. A burro brayed abrasively. Mother pig and her piglets grunted and squealed along the trail near our house, babies cried, our horse, King, nickered for his morning's ration of corn.

As we looked out our window, the brown thatched-roof huts were bathed in the soft, early light of dawn that hovered lightly over the landscape, diffused in a layer of fog mixed with smoke curling up from a myriad of small fires in huts where tortillas were baking on clay *comales* (griddles). The scene resembled an abstract, surreal Monet painting.

In the house next to us, Petra began the rhythmic pat-pat-pat ritual as she made the corn tortillas for the family breakfast. "Uncle Nick," our neighbor, liked to sing hymns lustily, especially at 5:00 a.m. as I frantically tried to get one more hour of beauty sleep. It would be all right if he didn't pitch the songs an octave too high. I felt like I had to reach those high notes for him.

A fatherless family of five children lived on the other side of us. Mother is my laundry-lady. Early in the morning before hiking to their fields, they liked to sing the Spanish choruses they learned at the little chapel. The women and girls began to laugh and chatter as they bustled around with meal preparation, fire-building and baby-tending. By 6:00 a.m., if I still

Life and Work in Mecayapan, Veracruz, Mexico

The women gracefully balance buckets of water on their heads as they walk home from the river.

---

insisted on staying in bed, I probably would be the last one up in the whole village.

The children have gradually gotten used to us. A few of them still stand around and watch us through the windows, sit quietly on our front bench, play with the plastic blocks or look at the books on the display table.

The neighbor kids were sometimes quite mischievous. They liked to turn on the water barrel faucet and then run away. If I closed the shutters on the back window by our bed they tried to push them open. In this culture respecting people's property and privacy was something they knew nothing about. As far as they were concerned, everything was open for inspection.

One day seven year old Victor and his mother walked to Soteapan and he came home sporting a new pair of shoes.

God's Talk

Early one morning he proudly paraded around our house clad only in a tattered, buttonless shirt and his new shoes! That afternoon we saw him down at the river and what was he doing? Carefully washing his new shoes, scrubbing each little crack vigorously with a handful of twigs. His mother wistfully reported the shoes cost 20 pesos ($2.50 US), a fantastic sum of money for a poverty-stricken widow. She said he had begged for a pair of shoes "like Carolina (Carrie) wears." Ironically, she begs to go barefooted like Victor does!

Other activities included inviting the pastor and his wife, who was near her delivery date, to have supper and an informal visit with us. They lost their first child so we prayed with them that this baby would be born healthy.

Ah, a quiet April evening to enjoy the stars, tropical balmy breezes and a full moon in the village of Mecayapan. Fires were visible on the distant hills where brush was being burned off to prepare for planting the new crops of corn and beans. As we walked around the village we greeted people chatting outside their huts, sitting on small stools, rustic chairs or a big boulder. Their dim outlines showed up against the dark wall or were silhouetted against the glow of the flickering fires inside the huts. The cool evenings bring soothing relief from the heat of the day. Children cavort in the moonlight and families visit till ten or eleven o'clock. There isn't a hint of fear here on a dark night. These are gentle people and many have believed, or at least are sympathetic to the Gospel.

The women were always terribly curious about the fact that I have only one child. Frequently I was asked if I take medicine so I don't have anymore children. I never could tell for sure if they envied me or pitied me! It seemed like one woman envied me because she asked if I could get her some medicine so she wouldn't have so many children. They have heard vague rumors about birth control pills. Some are bold enough to ask if I'd had an "operation."

Sunday evening. A south wind blew today that chased away the cold air we have felt for a week. The village drummer stands in the *kiosko* (gazebo), located in the middle of the town plaza, and beats out a code on his wood and leather drum calling for the village men to bring their machetes and cut the grass in the plaza. Kids' voices echo among the buildings. Chickens know which are their own trees in which to roost. Some are already up in the branches of the huge spreading mango tree next door.

Carl writes about firewood, green beans and red capsules:

> *Pablo Perez likes to go along with me to our market town. Sometimes we use his horse to carry cargo home from town to where our car is parked in Soteapan. Today, however, he said his horse is going to be used to make some* tomin *(money) hauling corn. So we'll have to limit our purchases to what we can carry on our backs over the trail.*

> *Coming home he pointed to a good-sized oak tree along the trail, "I killed that tree for firewood," he said. I noticed that the leaves were dried up and the trunk had been girdled with a cut several inches deep. I asked how one could know whose tree it was. Did he put his special mark on it? It's on an honor system -- no one else will touch a tree that has been killed or felled. It's understood. You fell your tree, you have it for your firewood.*

> *We hadn't been in the village very long when our good friend Chencho brought us something that he had discovered in the*

savanna, a small bottle with a rusty lid and illegible label that contained some red capsules, several cans of green beans and a mouse-infested pillow with chicken feathers still in it.

"I think an airplane must have dumped it," he said, "Do you think they are still good?"

"How rare!" I exclaimed, not giving a hint that I knew anything about them. "It could have been an airplane, yes. And no, I don't think they are good."

Chencho explained, "Other people have seen these things and won't go near the spot because they are afraid that the evil spirits must have dumped it all!" He no longer believes the traditions of evil spirits now that he's a Christian, so decided it must have been an airplane that dumped it.

I knew instantly that he had stumbled on to a bag of trash that I threw out after we cleaned out the house. I had carefully chosen what I thought was an isolated spot a long distance from the trail and had naively hoped no one would find them. I sure didn't want anyone to open them and eat the contents. Good grief! Those cans of beans were bulging, that's why we threw them out!

There is no place here to get rid of trash that appears to the people to have some value. If they observe someone throwing away valuable things, well, maybe you are so rich that you can throw money away too! We learned quickly that we are constantly under observation and rumors travel with lightning speed in this society!

In June 1966, on our return from a linguistic workshop, my neighbor brought over five big, juicy-ripe mangos from

Life and Work in Mecayapan, Veracruz, Mexico

the huge mango tree between her house and ours. They tasted so good for lunch, which we ate on the run because right away people came running to welcome us home. Elias brought us eggs. Chepa offered to carry water up from the *pozo* (water hole) to boil for drinking.

The house was in pretty good shape, just very dusty. Mice and rats had chewed holes through the mud walls so we set the traps again. Things were intact that we packed in tightly closed barrels and cans to prevent mice and cockroaches from getting in. We only needed to scrub table tops, chairs, shelves and sweep the dirt floor. I moved things gingerly, to avoid encountering "critter-friends" that might be lurking in the corners and calling this home now.

Pablo Perez, one of our nearest neighbors, often stopped to chat or help Carl with whatever he might be doing. Two years after we got acquainted, he and his wife began to study the Bible and believe in God's Way. They, along with their four bright eyed, mischievous children, attended the nightly services at the little church which Pablo helped to build. He had a growth in his eye that prevented him from reading, so we took him to the mission hospital in Puebla to have the growth surgically removed by a Christian doctor there. He was so glad when he could read the Bible verses we were translating!

Pablo was one of several men in the village who made men's shirts and full-cut trousers on a treadle sewing machine. Older village men wore the ample, baggy style of trousers with deep pockets that were handy for carrying things. One day a man came to our door with 8 eggs, 4 in each pocket. It wasn't at all obvious until he started pulling them out one by one! The younger fellows were requesting more styl-

God's Talk

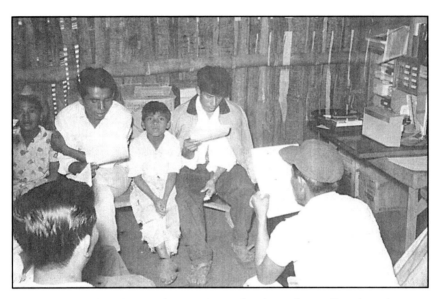

The men would gather in the evenings after long days of hard work to listen to recorded music and readings of scripture.

ish trousers so Pablo asked to borrow a pair of Carl's slim-legged trousers from which he could cut a pattern.

Some evenings 25-29 men and teenage fellows would come to study the booklets we displayed on the porch. They were an eager, lively group and we were glad they felt free to come. Occasionally someone came who had been drinking too much, but one of the others would ask him to leave. Sadly, many of the men struggled with alcohol that was so readily available.

The women and girls were more shy, but a few became brave enough to visit me. I went to their homes when there was sickness and often I went for a friendly visit to learn new vocabulary. Sylvia and Juanita were my faithful language helpers and helped me with cooking, housework and translation. They both made their own dresses on treadle machines without any pattern, just by guessing the size! I never could figure out how they did that.

One Sunday we were abruptly shaken out of our reveries when we suddenly heard lots of shouting, smelled smoke, and saw people running with buckets of water to our neighbor's house that was on fire next door. We joined in the pail parade but there was no hope of saving the burning house. Our efforts could maybe keep other houses from catching fire. It took only a few minutes for the flimsy stick-and-thatch structure to be in ruins. Soon we noticed hundreds of pesky cockroaches, threatened by the fire, make a beeline from the burned house to our house! We quickly dusted around the outside of our house with chlordane to kill or divert them on their journey.

The delicious, yeasty smell of fresh baked bread wafted our way from Uncle Nick's mud-brick oven next door to our house. I was usually one of his first customers for the crusty delicacies. He told me his wife used to be a "witch doctor" who was both feared and respected as one who knew many secrets pertaining to witchcraft and healing. For many years she resisted the Gospel to the point of making it hard for Uncle Nick to remain a radiant Christian. I had opportunities to speak to her about following God's Talk when she visited me. One day she told me she started attending the nightly services and was believing God's Talk. We rejoiced that she wanted to know more.

Let me introduce you to one of my littlest friends, three year old Larry (Hilario). He was such a cute kid! His mother, Rosa, had been my friend for a long time, but Larry recently realized that I was his friend, too. He was one of the few children whose mother has not threatened to take him to the foreign lady's house for an injection if he misbehaves! Many

God's Talk

Fresh bread from a mud oven was always a treat.

---

mothers warned their youngsters about the "white lady who eats children."

Little Larry stopped being my friend for about a week when his mother brought his baby brother for a penicillin injection. When the baby cried as I gave him the injection Larry became agitated. The second time he came, he brought a stick and started to hit me with it when I injected the baby. Several days later the baby recovered but Larry couldn't forgive me for what I'd done. He wouldn't smile, but instead would scowl fiercely and hit me if he could. He felt protective of his little brother.

Then one day Rosa came to visit me and asked if I would show her how to cook oatmeal and make chicken bouillon. (These two foods were readily available at the little local store, so I taught mothers these two bland foods are good for anyone who has intestinal problems or is dehydrated.) Larry, of course, came too and was keenly interested in all the proceedings. When it was taste time, he promptly devoured his oatmeal and soup. The baby, too, yelled for more in between bites, his mother couldn't feed it to him fast enough. All of a sudden I stopped being Larry's enemy and became his friend again. He lovingly came over next to me, put his soft, grubby little hand in mine, looked up and smiled sweetly as if to say, "I'm sorry. I thought you had stopped being my friend."

But the best was yet to come. Rosa's real reason for coming that day was to tell me that she and her husband, Moses, had recently believed in the Lord and she wanted to buy one of the Nahuatl hymn books and a copy of the book of Acts in Nahuatl to study. We joyfully hugged each other and I praised the Lord for His faithfulness in speaking to their hearts.

During our fifth year in the village, while on a home visit, I spied one of our missing stainless teaspoons. How did they get one of our spoons? I commented on the pretty spoon and was told they got it in Soteapan. Maybe they did buy it, who knows, but we were missing a spoon. It wasn't a good feeling to have something stolen, especially when it was part of a set. Should I say something? My first thought was it was not right to let them keep it. But, if we made a big thing of it, how would it look to people who have so little and see that we have so much in comparison? They had no concept of the value we place on having a complete set of spoons. Maybe they have no concept that stealing is wrong. Still, should we teach them it isn't right to steal? That is the only spoon they have in the house. The people eat with tortillas and fingers. We decided to let the matter rest, trusting they will come to know Christ's love sooner than if we asked for our spoon

God's Talk

back. After all, we have other spoons. Here's an idea, a Scripture Memory contest and give spoons for a reward!

Here's an example of greetings on the trail, a running commentary on the obvious:

> *As I huff and puff up the trail carrying two full buckets of clear, sparkling water, one in each hand. I meet my neighbor gracefully balancing a large basin full of laundry on her head:*
>
> *"Have you just come from getting water?" she says.*
>
> *"Yes," I say, "I've just come from getting water".*
>
> *I say, "Are you going to wash clothes?"*
>
> *"Yes, I'm going to wash clothes," she replies.*
>
> *Then we each go our own way.*

Transportation

In 1966 when our tourist visas were due for renewal, we went to visit Ernest and Betty Frey's family in Houston. Through a car dealer there we traded our 1955 Olds for a bright shiny red 1961 Ford Galaxie to drive back to Mexico. Papers for importing the car took longer than expected.

For our first several years there was no bridge over the big river between Mecayapan and the main highway. The unpaved, rough, rutty, muddy "road" was passable only with a cargo truck, and even then only during the dry season when the river was low. If we needed to buy supplies in Acayucan, our market town, we had to first hike the trail or bounce on a horse, scramble up slippery, rocky inclines, splash through rushing mountain streams, step cautiously on partially submerged boulders, and slide down the muddy trail to where our car was parked at the end of the paved road. From there it was wonderful to ride comfortably on the smooth, all-weather highway for the 50 miles to town.

Carl writes:

> *We knew that eventually we would need a more versatile vehicle when the bridge under construction over the big river would be completed and the road improved. So, in 1968 we bought a green '52 Chevy carry-all for $50 "as is" from E.W. Hatcher, the MAF pilot in Chiapas. It was already registered and licensed in Mexico and that saved me from having to go through gobs of red tape. His son Rodney drove it straight through from their Missionary Aviation Fellowship headquarters in Fullerton, California to Oklahoma City where I went to get it. I bought a set of tires for it, got the springs repaired and had another rear end put in. In Mexico old cars are kept running almost indefinitely. With all that expense, I soon ran out of money. Friends and relatives kindly gave me money gifts to help cover expenses for the trip back to Mexico City.*

During the next two years the carry-all allowed us to ford the Huasuntlan river at a low spot and drive right up to our front door in the village. We eagerly anticipated the day the bridge would be done so we wouldn't have to risk the swift current.

The narrow dirt road beyond the river was unimproved and in the rainy season we mired down in the sticky, clay-like mud more than once. Since the carry-all was so old we limited the amount of driving to short trips in that area and

God's Talk

Fording the river in the Chevy carry-all.

used the red Ford for long trips back and forth to the City and the States.

The Big Day finally came when the bridge was finished! On returning from a shopping trip, the Chevy roared right along, crossed over the bridge and bounced in over the ten miles of ruts that passed for a road all the way to our house. Warily we kept watching the storm clouds pile up over the mountains and arrived home only minutes before the torrents of rain poured down. We praised the Lord for holding off the rain long enough for us to arrive home without incident. Then it rained everyday for a week making the road impassable.

Communication with the Outside World

Some friends in Oklahoma City, Harry and Cindy Reeder, gave us two walkie-talkies to take along to Mexico, one for Linds and one for us. We weren't sure how far they would reach, but they served like telephones between our village and the Lind family's village in Ocotal Chico three miles away up the mountain. We arranged to talk each morning at 7:00 a.m. That was when there was the least interference. We called ourselves "banana grove" and Linds called themselves "little piney."

One of our church supporters gave us a good short-wave radio for listening to stations around the world, especially Christian stations like HCJB from Quito, Ecuador. We could keep up with what's going on in the outside world. In addition, we had a two-way radio that we used for daily contact (in Spanish) with our headquarters in Mexico City 500 miles northwest and also the SIL translation center and Missionary Aviation (MAF) in Oaxaca 300 miles to the west. This provided an important link with the Wycliffe translators' "party line" from Chiapas to Mexico City. MAF pilots in Oaxaca used our weather reports each morning -- whatever weather we reported they could expect 24 hours later. They could plan their flights accordingly out to the translators' village locations in Oaxaca. One of the men helped Carl put up two 35 foot bamboo poles for attaching the radio antenna. This allowed us to get a lot more stations on our short-wave radio. With all these technological wonders, we felt much less isolated.

Once or twice a week a second-class bus delivered mail to Soteapan, the small village at the end of the paved road where we parked our car. Don Adolfo kindly kept mail for us at his store until we picked it up which was about every two weeks. Occasionally, the town officials would hand-carry our mail over the foot trail and deliver it to us personally as a favor. We appreciated them doing that for us. It was unsafe and impractical to send packages to us directly through the mail. One package we received had obviously been opened and several things confiscated by customs officials.

How Carrie Adjusted

My neighbor lady often took Carrie along to the river to wash our clothes. She soon became acquainted with the other children and liked to spend time swimming and playing at the river with them. She learned to swim quite well and never lacked for playmates.

Before we built the bath addition to our outhouse, the two of us took daily trips to the river for baths. The sun was so warm and comforting, a good antidote when I would sometimes feel depressed. After that relaxation, I always felt more cheerful.

She developed an ear infection from the contaminated river water but it cleared up with medication. Her legs had infected insect bites where she scratched them. She constantly begged to go barefooted. I finally allowed it after emphasizing how important it was to stay on the dry, beaten paths to avoid hookworm parasites that live in soft moist earth and enter the body through the feet.

The music and story records she played repeatedly also entertained her and her friends who came around to play. They memorized some of the words and music so we were amused to hear the neighbor children sing "Oh, say but I'm glad, I'm glad..." and they didn't understand a word of it! She liked to trot after her daddy while he worked around the house and I loved having her beside me helping while I baked our weekly bread. As she got older she made pancakes sometimes. As an adult she baked lots of bread for her own family.

Sometimes she went to someone's house and one of her friends would pick her hair over for head lice, which was what the women did for each other. Carrie was pleased that she had *atins* (lice) like her friends have! Mother wasn't pleased, though.

Carrie loved animals and just couldn't keep away from a horse. She begged for a horse or burro. Being an only child probably increased her fascination for pets, and horses especially. One day she fell off a horse and hurt her arm so badly we thought it might be broken. After we splinted and bandaged it Carl took her to Acayucan to have it X-rayed and found it wasn't broken. The doctor didn't charge for his services, but instead said, "We need more people like you who are helping our country, and I want to do this for you." How generous of him! At least one person in this country didn't take us for all we've got because he thought we were "rich Americans." This was our first contact with him, but he had heard about what we were doing. Carl brought the X-rays back with him and showed them to our visitors that evening. Not knowing what X-rays were, they were impressed and amazed it was Carrie's bones they were looking at.

On her 13th birthday she was thrilled when she could buy her own horse with money she had saved, a two-year old filly that she trained to ride.

Other pets she acquired along the line (not all at one time) were baby rabbits, kittens, a puppy, tadpoles, baby chicks and lightning bugs which she kept it in a jar and played with until they finally died. She promptly named her two baby rabbits John and Mary. How original.

One day she got scissors-happy and snipped off patches of her puppy's fur! She tried to cover up her mischief by saying, "Mommy, a whole big bunch of the puppy's fur fell out when it was just sitting on my lap!" At first I only said "Oh?" and didn't look very close but upon closer inspection it was obviously done with a sharp instrument. Poor thing, it sure looked moth-eaten.

Language Acquisition and Play

Her days were full of learning two languages. She learned Nahuatl right along with us. In fact, when she started talking Nahuatl in her sleep, we knew she was absorbing it into her subconscious. She eventually spoke the language fluently with the girls her age. It was so cute to hear them chatter as they jumped rope using jungle vines, played house in an improvised shelter they built under the trees using rocks, leaves and sticks for furniture, smoothed out a place to make mud "pies" and "tortillas," swam in the river and climbed trees.

Carrie's Schooling and Social Opportunities

WBT teachers developed a good home-school curriculum that was used at all three workshop centers, Ixmiquilpan, Mitla and Mexico City. Parents who taught their children out in the remote villages could keep up with their peers at any of those locations. Our family usually spent at least three months at a time at linguistic or translation workshops and Carrie could attend school there along with other translators' children.

She was the only girl in her kindergarten class at Ixmi but she had a bike to ride, trees to climb and a big furry dog named Osito to romp with. The 20 children had wonderful times together. The workshop center had twelve duplexes and a study building that encircled a large grassy area where they could safely play games and get healthy exercise. This allowed us parents the freedom to concentrate on translation. I gave Carrie piano lessons as well.

The piñata party, a traditional Mexican game, was a big hit with everyone. Everybody cheered! Starting with the youngest, each child in turn was blindfolded and given a big stick. The goal was to hit the piñata suspended from a rope held by a person at each end. These two people would swing the piñata back and forth making it difficult for the blindfolded child to know where to swing the stick at it. The children squealed with delight when an older child succeeded in hitting the piñata hard enough to shatter it and everyone scrambled for the goodies as they scattered on the grass. Carrie got a chance to hit the gaily decorated clay pot filled with candy, cookies and gum.

She did great in her village studies all through seventh grade, using lesson plans developed for the home school curriculum by our Wycliffe teachers. I found it a challenge to teach science and learn about all the things that weren't yet discovered when I was in elementary school. I learned as much as she did. Some days it was more difficult to concentrate because of loud music playing from the taverns and other interruptions, but we kept to the schedule pretty well. When Juanita Lind lived with us for a few weeks, she taught Carrie Spanish, reading and spelling. Having more than one teacher all day long gave her a break from mother's supervision.

Volunteer Wycliffe school teachers lived with us for six weeks at three different times to give Carrie a break from my homeschooling. Ruth Ann Price in 1972, Betty Huizenga in 1969 and Dan Hoopert in 1974. We appreciated their dedicated service so much. When we moved to Texas in 1974 and she enrolled in public school 8th grade, she was right up with her grade level. That was gratifying to all of us.

A Few of Her Cute Sayings

We were sure that our daughter must be normal because she did what the books say little girls do about age five or six. She took a special liking to her daddy and announced one day, "I'm going to marry my daddy when I grow up."

At the early age of five she cut out a picture of Jesus from an old calendar and said, "Mother, I want to paste this up somewhere so people can see it and celebrate God and the Bible." It was heart-warming and rewarding to think that even at that tender age she was able to grasp why we were there and shared our sense of mission.

One evening as she was getting ready for bed, suddenly she said quite emphatically, "I sure wish the people wouldn't spit on our floor!" I said "It's a custom they have because they have dirt floors in their houses and they haven't been taught anything different. I don't know how we could get them to stop." She immediately piped up with "I know how they could. They could just swallow it." Good idea! We wish it were that easy, but I guess we'll have to go the long way around and teach them why they shouldn't spit in public places.

As most children do, Carrie counted the days until Christmas. She asked so often that I finally put up a string of safety pins, and each day she removed one, and counted how many were left (a device we nurses used to count the days before graduation from nursing school). It must be very painful for a child to learn to WAIT. We worked together to make simple Christmas decorations with locally available supplies.

Many times I wished her grandparents could hear her excitedly relate some happening of the day. Her sparkling brown eyes fairly danced with exuberance and enthusiasm. The pictures we took don't show the seven cute little freckles on her nose! She often wiggled her front teeth to check if they were beginning to come loose. One night when I was putting her to bed she said, "Mother, I sure wish we were in Heaven. There we won't have to go to bed!!"

When our 80-year-old friend Flora visited us, she showed us how adaptable she was by eating burned, crisp, or dried food, even old dried out tortillas dipped in coffee. Carrie was impressed. So one day when the cornbread burned on the bottom, I trimmed it off. Carrie said, "Let's send a package of the burned part in a letter to Flora!" I said, "Flora will like if I write and tell her what you said." Carrie piped up, "I guess she'd really be giggled to get a package of burned cornbread." Then Carrie, the kitty and Silvia proceeded to eat all the burnt trimmings!

Once she made a pronouncement. "Mommy, when I grow up I think I know what I want to be..." I held my breath wondering if she had changed her mind about being a "missionary nurse like mommy so I can help people." "I decided I want to be a missionary dancer!" Blow me over, where did she ever get that idea? When I asked her, she nonchalantly said, "Oh, I just now made it up!" She "made up" lots of things. Like questions about babies and how they begin. One day, after a thoughtful pause in her stream of chatter, she asked her daddy, "What kind of animal would it make if a daddy kitty put his seed in a mama dog?" Ah sweet innocence!

God's Talk

When Carl brought home a jar of real Yucatan hot sauce, I made the remark, "It is so hot we'll use only a drop at a time and it will last forever." Carrie piped up and said, "Maybe it will last till I get married!"

She was working on some embroidery and suddenly said, "When I grow up I'm going to be a Ladies Aid. That's a good thing to be, isn't it? 'Cause that's the way you can use your hands to serve Jesus." She remembered when the Ladies' Aid at our home church made dresses for us one summer.

Food We Ate, Cooked, and Baked

For two years I cooked on the three-burner kerosene stove the Laws left. It had a square, removable oven that did a passable job on some things. Then another translator couple, Paul and Dorothy Smith, gave us their apartment-size butane gas stove with a real honest-to-goodness oven. They had it shipped to our market town and we had it hauled in with Fred's truck. With a lot of elbow-power, Carrie, our visiting friend, Flora, and I scrubbed off the film of grease and dirt until it looked and worked like new. Now I could bake in a real oven.

Butchering Day. Fred was one of the few townspeople who could afford to own cattle. Every two or three weeks he butchered one of them, starting about 4:00 a. m. He hoisted the carcass up on a frame and then he chopped off big chunks of meat with a machete, no neatly carved steaks or roasts for sale. We had to get there early if we wanted any: it was first-come first-served.

Carl always went over early to be sure to get good fresh beef. After not having fresh meat for a couple of weeks, he bought a half kilo (one pound) of liver. We were so hungry we ate it all for dinner with onions and potatoes. Delicious! I canned six pints of stew meat in the pressure cooker. We had a meat grinder for hamburger so I canned hamburger patties in glass jars. They tasted wonderful with fresh baked buns! Meat loaf, Italian spaghetti, chili or sloppy joes also added variety to our diet.

Occasionally our monthly check from Mexico City headquarters was delayed, causing us to run low on money to buy food and supplies in our market town. At times like that my ingenuity was tested on meal preparation. We never went hungry. People often gifted us with corn tortillas, eggs, beans, rice, fresh tropical vegetables and fruit from their fields. It was usually a friendly gesture but sometimes it was payment for medicines. We could live a long time on those staples.

Tropical taste treats tickled our taste buds. A unique tropical fruit is called *totot tzapo'* in Nahuatl, *anona* in Spanish and soursop in English. It is the size of a large coconut and has a tough green knobby skin. Inside is a smooth, buttery consistency, with bland, slightly sweet flavor that resembles pureed pears. Carrie loved to roll the shiny slippery seeds around in her mouth before spitting them out.

Early on we planted an avocado seed in our yard. The tree grew rapidly and produced bumper crops in June each year. We pigged out on them while they lasted. I made delicious watermelon pickles with the rinds of a watermelon someone gave us. Stalks of bananas grew on the banana plants outside our back door. I could whip up a banana cake in jig time. Wild grapes grew profusely in the mountains. One of the villagers brought some to my door so I bought them and made six pints of delicious jelly.

God's Talk

A surprise feature in our diet one day came in the form of a live female iguana. It measured about three feet long from teeth to tail. When someone brought it to us, I had no idea what to do with this strange looking animal. Pastor John said his wife knew how to cook it. I said we'd buy it if she'd fix it and we could enjoy it together. As she cleaned and cut it up, inside this ugly, menacing looking creature were 28 white, soft, leathery, tough-shelled eggs, about the size of a ping pong ball. She cooked everything in a spicy tomato sauce, including the eggs!! We tasted it gingerly, cautiously. Surprise! It tasted like chicken and the eggs had a delicate flavor that made us want more! Carrie ate 8 eggs herself, besides two pieces of meat. All agreed it was nice to say we have eaten it, but weren't sure we'd exchange it for beef, chicken or pork. The meal was topped off with shoo-fly pie. Tongue in cheek, Carl said his favorite meal always was iguana stew and shoo-fly pie.

Carrie had her own unique tastes, too. Forget about German chocolate cake! Give her sour plums, salted green mangos, *pozol* (corn gruel), burnt corn, beans and tortillas. Also toasted locusts! At a certain time of year the enormous locusts emerged from their cocoons in the ground. The locusts then flew half-way up on the sides of the trees where they were practically invisible to untrained eyes. She and her village friends easily spotted them with their keen, practiced eyes. They put sticky tree resin on the tips of long grass flower spines which they used to reach up and touch the locusts. The locusts would stick to the gooey resin. Then they pulled the locust off the resin and popped it in a little bag. When each child had collected enough locusts, they carried them home to toast on a *comal* (clay griddle), sprinkled them with salt and chowed down on them, crispy and crunchy, better than potato chips or Fritos!

The children collected small fresh-water crabs hidden under stones in the stream bed. One day, Carrie brought ten crabs home and plopped them on the hot clay griddle to toast. One brave crab took off running and crawled under the stove top. (We can't blame him!) I forgot about it until bedtime when I noticed something crawling on the floor. Here was this poor crab, minus two legs. I exclaimed, "Oh that's the crab that got away!" Carrie, having been in bed a half hour, was almost asleep. Well, whadaya know? When she heard my exclamation, she climbed down from her bed in the loft, caught the doomed crab, washed, toasted and ate it, then went back to bed. What a delicious bedtime delicacy it must have been!

During our first eight years in the village, we had no way to keep food cold so it required a whole different way of meal-planning, cooking and storing food. Left-over food had to be eaten the next meal. We had some interesting menus for breakfast! We could buy whole powdered milk in one-gallon tin cans with tight lids. I would make up small amounts of milk at a time to avoid spoilage. When empty, the cans were excellent for storage to prevent the ever-pesky cockroaches from gaining access.

All of us learned to be resourceful and make do with whatever was available. Since we had no way to refrigerate anything, Carl made an ice chest out of a steel army trunk the Laws had left. He first lined it with one-inch styrofoam and then covered that with galvanized sheet metal. Later on, when we were able to drive our carry-all in to the village, we took this "ice chest" with us to our market town and brought home a 100 pound block of ice. Then we could keep fresh meat, veggies and milk cold for up to four days.

God's Talk

While visiting our home church on furlough in 1971, one of the farm couples there heard me say that we drank warm Pepsi because we had no refrigerator. Ilene told me later she couldn't stand the thought of us drinking warm Pepsi! She exclaimed, "Norm has to have his Pepsi ice cold so I take it to him in the field in a bucket of ice. How could we get a refrigerator to you?" Within the next few months they located a butane gas refrigerator and shipped it to Laredo, Texas. We picked it up there and hauled it in a borrowed trailer over the 1000 miles back to the village. Since tanks of butane gas were cheap and easily accessible in our market town, we had it set up and running in record time. Like curious children, we eagerly checked every hour or so to see if ice cubes were freezing yet. Sure enough, three hours later ice cubes were clinking in our glasses of Pepsi and we actually had congealed Jello for dessert. Occasionally we made small batches of ice cream in the freezer. Thank you, Ilene and Norm Holt. What a lovely gift you gave us!

Each day was packed full to the brim for me: prepare meals, help Juanita make a dress, coach Sylvia on her knitting, teach Carrie her home-school lessons, treat people's ailments, make house-calls, learn more new words in Aztec, write letters, mend clothes, type manuscripts, etc. Endless tasks, it seemed. I was often so tired I was in bed at 8 o'clock! With so many things to think about and keep in order, I wondered sometimes how I kept my thoughts together enough to get an edible meal together.

I almost didn't one day. I bought a scrawny chicken for 10 pesos (80 cents U.S.), cleaned it and put it on to cook, hoping to fix it Aztec-style by first cooking it whole, then put it on a stick and brown it over hot coals. It dawned on me fifteen minutes into cooking that I forgot to take the insides out. Yikes! Quickly I fished it out of the water. In that short length of time it had barely gotten warm, so no harm done. I gutted the insides and boiled it for an hour but it never did get very tender. Oh, well...

When the Linds came down the mountain from their village to spend a day with us, we savored spaghetti and meatballs, buttered green beans, raisin pie and coffee. Oh, yes, and homemade bread with wild grape jelly. Mmmm!

Some days when I felt nostalgic, I fixed a real American-style dinner, hamburgers (canned) on fresh-baked hamburger buns with any trimmings I might have on hand: sliced tomato, onion, mustard, catsup, mayonnaise, hot sauce. What taste-treats! Royce Lind brought me some sausage seasoning when they returned from the States. The next time a pig was butchered I added some to the meat and we had good spicy sausage with our eggs!

Marilyn writes:

> *Today for the first time Carrie and I were invited to eat with a group of women who were cooking a meal for the men replacing the thatch roof on the pastor's house. A big kettle of* mole, *pronounced MO-ley, (pork gravy) simmered over an open fire and two women patted out tortillas. We joined in eating native style using a tortilla instead of a spoon to dip into the gravy. Very tasty! Much smacking of lips and licking the fingers. Naturally we wondered how many "bugs" we were ingesting. People were always so eager to show hospitality that it would be totally unthinkable to refuse to eat what was served due to fear of bugs. We'd deal with any bugs later.*

God's Talk

A sampling of local native foods we enjoyed:

Fresh-water crabs, chipilin, freshwater snails, quilite, iguana, corn, locusts, tomatoes, freshwater shrimp, squash flowers, sweet potatoes, coffee, yucca, black beans, guanabana, coyolin, mamey, avocado, mango, papaya, oranges, cho'no'no', acoyo, bananas, coconuts, pineapple, limones, epazote, squash.

Fighting the Critters: Rats, Scorpions, Ticks, et al

One day while we were hunting for something, a huge tarantula crawled out of the laundry bag, -- a big, hairy, ugly black one. He (or was it she?) ended up in a tightly closed jar of alcohol. It still sends shivers up my spine just to think about it.

As I was typing away on the health book manuscript one afternoon, I noticed a moving object on the floor. A large scorpion was casually meandering along. It didn't take long for him to be incarcerated too! Wonder what we'll encounter next? UGH!

Ticks were an ever-present plague when we hiked over the jungle trails. Somehow they always managed to lodge on our bodies in the most inconvenient places such as the groin and armpits! When we tried to remove them, they dug in deeper. And oh how they itched! Biting fleas were equally obnoxious and caused severe itching and open sores. When we took Scripture portions to other villages and stayed overnight in people's huts, we fought with both fleas and bedbugs that nearly ate us alive!

Life and Work in Mecayapan, Veracruz, Mexico

Carl writes about our rat troubles:

Right from the beginning of our life here, we had huge rat troubles. The rats thought they were welcome here and made themselves right at home. I sure had news for them! I spent nearly half a day making a contraption that would trap the rat when he pulled on the bait. In a short amount of time we buried 29 rats and I don't know how many mice!

Another rat trap that worked well was one with a door that dropped the rat into a can of water and drowned the creature. When people wanted to start a concerted effort against the plague of rats in the village we bought a dozen or more good sturdy traps which we loaned out for a week to anyone who wanted to use one. The people were grateful for any help to get rid of them because they nibbled away at their winter corn supply.

You would wince if you could see some of the other wicked-looking traps he rigged up! There must have been millions of rats in a village of this size. They multiplied and spread disease faster than we could eliminate them. Our guerrilla warfare on the rats and mice continued the whole time we lived here. Later on we've described how the DDT spray for mosquitoes caused the rat population to multiply.

Our Garden

Being avid gardeners, one of our first projects was to fence in a garden plot next to the house where we could plant flowers and vegetables. Lemon-grass plants and banana shoots grew to maturity in one year. We planted sweet corn, lettuce, cucumbers, squash, tomatoes, four coconut palms, an avocado tree from one seed, a mango tree, hibiscus plants,

God's Talk

an orange tree, papaya plant, poinsettias and other tropical plants. A year later it looked like a tropical garden! Everything elicited excited comments by the women as they walked by our garden on their way to the river and by the men during their evening visits.

The hibiscus bloomed profusely with big salmon-colored flowers. The banana plants gave us several huge stalks of bananas. The tall, flavorful lemon-grass made a delicious hot or cold drink. Zeke brought us eight pineapple plants from his *milpa* (field) so they went in our garden along with the four from pineapples we had eaten. Just cut off the pineapple tops, stick them in the ground and they start to grow!

What a beautiful sight our tomato patch was, 15 lovely big plants with huge tomatoes hanging on. We had fun giving them away. People came from all over town to admire them and talk about what we did to get them to produce that way. We told them that we dug horse manure into the soil before planting them. This custom was not familiar to them, though there were plenty of horses and donkeys in the village. This demonstration of the value of fertilizer inspired several to use it to increase their crops of corn, beans, coffee, pineapple and bananas. Our neighbor Peter was interested in the fertilizer idea. He made a nice fenced-in garden with cabbage, tomatoes, red beets, cantaloupes, zucchini squash and other vegetables. A few others also caught this idea.

Laundry

Twice a week my neighbor lady would take our laundry to wash on the rocks in the river. I gladly accepted her generous offer and paid her for it. She or her older daughter did it faithfully all the years we were there. From my perspective, it was hard back-breaking work to scrub dirty clothes on the big boulders in the middle of the river at the bottom of the hill. After scrubbing with soap powder, she would slap them on the rocks with a loud crack. I was amazed how clean the clothes were when she was finished. I was surprised they didn't seem to wear out any faster as a result of all the friction. She spread them out to dry on the bushes near the river or on our garden fence.

House Helpers

Silvia and Juanita were my faithful language assistants at different times. They also helped with cooking and housework. Both were fifteen-year-old Christian girls of marriageable age so I hoped they would find Christian husbands. Silvia, especially, was patient with me in language assimilation as we did housework together. She gained good experience, was able to go ahead with many things around the house. and we felt comfortable together. I learned a lot listening to her carry on an animated conversation with people when we visited together in homes. Juanita could read and write enough to help me write a health education booklet in Nahuatl.

Malaria Prevention

The Mexican government had an anti-malaria spraying program every six months. A crew of men came around with DDT and sprayed every house inside and outside with this foul-smelling chemical. All the furniture had to be taken out of the houses so they could spray under the roof, around the rafters, on every wall and on the floors, anywhere mosquitoes might lurk. It was a good chance to rearrange and clean in the corners, sort of like spring and fall housecleaning!

God's Talk

Tragically, after the sprayers go through the village, when the cats lick their paws, it isn't long until they go into convulsions and die. Then the rat and mice population proliferates and other diseases such as typhus, typhoid and parasites are allowed to flourish! Can't win for losing, as they say! We always used mosquito nets over our beds even though everything was sprayed with DDT.

Visitors We Hosted: Local People

The children came to see what strange things we might be doing. We changed our evening schedule to avoid being interrupted while eating our supper since the visitors would come about 6:00 p. m. We decided to eat a light snack about 5:00 p.m. and then again around 8:00 p.m. after we closed the door. This way we could devote all our time to whoever came to visit. Actually this was the Mexican custom for the evening meal.

We laid out various kinds of books for the adults and children to look at. We put out a few toys for the kids to play with. At home they may have had some crude homemade toys to play with. They liked the little plastic squares to fit together. Our book "All Around Us" had pictures of things they were familiar with. It was an excellent way to prepare them for reading some day and for us to learn vocabulary. We took notes and listened closely to their excited comments. The older girls chattered as they thumbed through the Sears catalogue, awed by the fashionable dresses, hair styles and shoes! As far as I could tell, the women didn't care about books. Their focus was on keeping their families fed, clean and clothed. Since many people still guessed time only by the position of the sun, some of the men asked Carl to teach them how to tell time with a clock or watch. He used a little book that had a small clock with movable hands.

Life and Work in Mecayapan, Veracruz, Mexico

You should have seen 14 little kids' eyes sparkle with anticipation and curiosity when I popped corn one evening. They had never seen it being popped before. I gave each of them a bag of popped corn that they snarfed down in a jiffy.

About noon one day three university students from Mexico City stopped to visit us. They were in the area to serve in a type of Mexican Peace Corps. One was studying to be a veterinarian and the other a mechanical engineer. The third one was their guide. Seemed like nice fellows. Carl invited them for dinner and they ate heartily! They asked questions about the Bible so we had a chance to talk with them about spiritual things.

One year at Christmas our visitors were intensely curious about the aluminum foil "icicles" Carrie had made for decorations. She hung them on the little hand-made tree and around the fireplace. We showed them some snow and ice pictures in the "All Around Us" book. They had never seen snow before. They stayed and talked around the fireplace until 9:30 that night, and listened to us tell about the customs and geography of our country.

It was New Year's Day, 1967. Several men chatted with Carl on the porch when the subject drifted to how the astronauts were preparing for a trip to the moon, which they heard about on Spanish news radio. He used the simplest possible vocabulary to explain intergalactic rockets. Their reaction was a mixture of amazement and utter disbelief that such a feat could ever be accomplished.

About 6:15 p.m. that evening more men and boys joined the group around our simple fireplace. The fire crackled pleasantly, casting a soft light on the eager, brown faces in a semi-circle as conversation drifted from subject to subject.

God's Talk

Carl read some translated Scripture from I John 1:9-12 and an animated discussion followed, some in Nahuatl and some in Spanish. Who can help but learn the Nahuatl language under such congenial circumstances?

Everyone cheered when I brought on the popcorn and a bag of marshmallows to toast over the fire. They weren't sure about the marshmallows, something entirely new to them. But after the first fellow gingerly tried one, he gave his vote of approval and everyone else joined in with enthusiastic oh's and ah's of enjoyment.

A young fellow who had taken a typing course in Acayucan came nearly every evening to practice typing in Spanish on our typewriter while his curious, admiring friends and casual on-lookers stood around to watch him. He actually did very well.

New Year's Day

There was a palpable air of festivity throughout the village as family groups prepared the traditional New Year tamale feasts. Some visitors often came bearing two or three of the big rounded, slightly sweet tamales with a bit of shredded beef or pork in the middle. Sometimes they were so big we had more than we could eat! What would be ahead for our friends in this New Year? For us? Only God knew what the coming year would be like.

Life and Work in Mecayapan, Veracruz, Mexico

Carl writes about literacy:

Frequently a visitor would bring a radio for me to repair. It was a good way to meet a felt need in the community. I always did like to tinker with things, take them apart, figure out how they work and put them back together again.

Tuesday evening.

A large group of visitors sat on the porch listening to Chencho, pastor of one of the small groups, as he and I studied the Bible. Celerino sat at the edge of the group with his copy of the Spanish Scriptures in his hands and was following along. He was intoxicated and called me **hermano** *(brother). I wonder what his history is. I'll ask him sometime if he wants to commit his life to Christ. He needs a Higher Power -- alcohol has such a powerful hold on some of these men.*

Two men from the Aztec village of Naranjo, part of a small group of believers in that town, came to ask me if I would help them learn how to read. They had come to buy Scriptures in Nahuatl and to invite us to come to their town and teach more people about God's Talk. They could read a little Spanish so I coached them in how to read Nahuatl, too. This pleased them very much. (We planned a trail trip over there which we have written about under "trail trips.")

As people learned to know us better, twenty or more visitors would sit on our porch while others stood around the porch rail, listening to the Gospel records, songs and translated Bible stories I read to them. The Lord was working in hearts and lives in a very wonderful way.

God's Talk

Fernando, Benito, Bartolo and Bonifacio picked up one of Carrie's books in English and tried to pronounce the words. I showed them the Nahuatl-Spanish-English phrase booklet I had recently made to explain how they could actually speak some English words and phrases. Bartie read several pages out loud and was so proud of himself.

Benny exclaimed that Carrie knew how to read. I said her mother teaches her every day. He said here people believe a parent shouldn't teach a child to read. It's not good, they said, only a teacher can do that.

The subject of a dictionary came up so I showed him my Spanish-English one from the shelf. He asked, " What are dictionaries for?" As he looked through the book he didn't know which way to go from where the book was open at M. It's difficult to comprehend what it must be like to not know how to read! After all, I've known how to read since I was six years old!

At first the women and girls were very shy. A few visited me often enough to get acquainted. I made lots of home visits when someone was sick, or for friendly visits and exposure to the language of their daily lives. The youngest children nearly always cried when mothers brought them to visit me. I was told that when they were naughty at home mother would scold them, "You better be good or the white lady will eat you!" They nearly always stopped crying when I reassured them in Nahuatl, "Don't be afraid, I won't eat you."

Celebrating!

After Chencho had been a believer for 17 years, he wanted to commemorate his acceptance of the Gospel. He had helped Howard Law on Scripture translation and the Gospel began to take root in his heart. He was the first person in Mecayapan who chose to believe God's Talk and he has served Him faithfully ever since, leading others to Christ. He and his family planned for two big celebration days at his house to include believers and non-believers. They graciously invited us to join in the festivities along with 200 or more people there. I took balloons over for all the kids and what a blast they had playing with them.

To protect the large crowd in case of rain, a large canvas awning was erected under the trees beside their thatch roof hut. Several women were busy grinding corn and patting out tortillas on their *metates* (grinding stones) that were brought over. Small fires on the ground heated the clay *comals* (griddles) set over three large stones. The tortillas were baked on the hot comals. One of the women stirred a big kettle of pork gravy that bubbled over a larger open fire.

We offered overnight accommodations to the out-of-town believers. Three families slept on their straw mats on our concrete living room floor and up in the *tapanco* (loft) -- 16 all together, six adults and 10 kids. Such a night of coughing, baby crying and people chattering! Even so, it was a blessed time for all to witness God's faithfulness among this wonderful group of God's people.

Stateside Visitors

Howard and Joan Law along with daughter Susan arrived safely July 20, 1966 for a week's visit with their many Aztec friends after being away ten years. Lots of visitors came to see them at our house. It was wonderful having them there.

Some of the changes Howard and Joan saw: the women and girls were not as shy and withdrawn; more older teen-age girls were going to school and waiting longer to get married;

God's Talk

a newly married couple moved into their own house right away instead of the cultural tradition of living with the boy's parents the first year so she could learn how to cook for him like his mother does.

The night before the Laws left, Chencho and his family came over to pray. It was like music to our ears when he prayed in Nahuatl. He ended with, "Now Lord, that's all I have to say so I'm going to stop." So natural and spontaneous!

In October 1967, our good friend, Flora Lewis from California, met us in Mexico City and spent two weeks in the village with us. Flora was 80 years old at the time, and was quite a trooper, impressed with all the different village sights, sounds and smells.

The large gathering of believers celebrates the Gospel's acceptance among the Aztec people.

I had hoped to relax in the hammock one warm Saturday afternoon when five Dutch young people who spoke excellent English hiked into town and walked right up to our house, two women and three fellows. They were on a four-day leave from their studies in the state capitol of Jalapa. They didn't expect it would take so long to get to the village. Since it was late in the day, they stayed long enough for us to visit over coffee and cookies. It had just rained and I felt sorry they had to hike back again over the slippery trail in the dark. Life had many surprises for us along the way and we never knew who would turn up in this neck of the woods!

Volunteers Come to Help

In July 1967 Ed Curtis and Howard Taylor, college-age men from Dallas Theological Seminary and Bob Jones University respectively, spent a month with us. They were with Practical Missionary Training to get first hand experience of missionary activity before they committed themselves to a mission board. They were very easy to get along with, eager for any new experiences and not fussy about eating new foods even if they thought it looked gross!

They told us missionary life wasn't at all like they expected. Not all glamorous and warm fuzzies like people in the states think of it. Many have pre-conceived ideas about what it is that missionaries do and what it's like to live on the mission field. Ed said he couldn't believe the huge amount of interruptions we had. He mentioned. "You just can't let yourself get shook if you don't get everything done in a day that you would like." He noted that it required intentionality and self-discipline to accomplish anything in the moments when no one was there asking for medicine or to buy books. So true!

God's Talk

For four weeks, Ed and Howard helped with various projects around the house: made a door for the shower stall, put a shelf in the outhouse, replaced wire on the oak fence, made a swing for the children, repaired a chair, put a roof gutter on the west side of the house, made new supporting beams through the center of house, accompanied me on house calls and filed vocabulary data in our shoebox. Carl took them on a hike which they enjoyed, through the jungle down to the big Huasuntlan Falls.

The next summer Jim Jorgenson and Steve Pitts came to learn all they could about missions in a remote area and help out on projects we had for them to tackle. It was a joy to have Jim and Steve there for such a good time of fun and fellowship. They too had a genuine desire to experience everything new, like give injections, build mud walls, bake biscuits, eat new foods, butcher chickens, watch the neighbor butcher his cow at 4:00 a.m., hike around the village to practice their language skills with the people. They helped us alphabetize language data, typed a clean copy of the newly translated book of Acts, and put a new door at the clinic entrance.

In November 1973, Dr. Bob Chen, volunteer from Houston, Texas, spent four weeks with us in the village. Thanks to Dr. Bob, I had an intensive refresher course in diagnostic procedures and pharmacology. He sutured several serious machete lacerations. I appreciated his help so much. He was familiar with tropical diseases and could help me diagnose and treat the more difficult cases: amebic dysentery, intestinal parasites, and tuberculosis. There were more cases of tuberculosis than I had seen in previous years. For most of the patients it was nearly impossible to make the 90 mile round-trip by bus to the nearest public X-ray facilities. Free medicines were available at the public health hospital if they could get there for that first diagnostic work-up. We personally took a few of the sicker patients in our carry-all to the Public Health Hospital in Minatitlan and then monitored their medications at home.

Colleagues Visit

We were encouraged when our administrators came to visit us in the village because we often felt isolated as we were the only Americans in this area. Frank Robbins, our Mexico Branch Director, his wife Ethel and their four children blessed us with an overnight visit on their way to visit other translation teams. Calvin Rensch, administrative assistant, and his wife Carolyn, John Alsop, our associate director, and his wife, Jean, all visited us at different times. They reassured us that we had a supportive team behind us.

George and Mary Huttar with daughter Heidi stopped by on their way back to the states after their Jungle Camp training was over. They gladly accepted my invitation to share our dinner of beef roast with potatoes, carrots and onions around it, tossed salad, ice cream and peanuts. When I put the roast in the oven, I thought: This is much more than we'll eat, maybe someone will come who would relish a meal. We were reminded of how starved we were for just such a meal when we got out of Jungle Camp five years before! Sure enough, they had hearty Jungle Camper appetites!

Our Medical and Dental Needs

We were so fortunate that we had no major extended illness while we lived in the village. From time to time Carrie had sores and fungus behind her ear, infected insect bites on her arms and legs, lice in her hair and intestinal worms that all responded to treatment. She kept me busy treating all her ailments.

Two weeks before our first Christmas in 1965 Carl became very sick with fever, diarrhea and vomiting. I treated him for typhoid and he responded well to Chloromycetin, the medication specific for typhoid. After bedrest and fluids for several days he began to feel better. In fact, Christmas Day he felt good enough to ride horseback over the trail to our car in Soteapan. We had been invited to spend the holiday with Baptist missionaries, Bert and Jean Fairweather, who lived in Acayucan. It was **so** good to be with like-minded friends with whom we could speak English. We didn't have to spend Christmas weekend just looking at each other or our neighbors.

In February 1968, while we were at a linguistic workshop at Ixmiquilpan, Carl ended up in the hospital in Mexico City for an appendectomy. Sure was a new experience for us! Our translation helper was able to work with the language project on his own until Carl was back home.

In 1969 it turned out that I had thyroiditis. Thankfully I didn't have to be hospitalized. Medication gradually brought me back to normal functioning.

In 1972 while we were in the village, Carl suffered severe pain in the lower back that was so painful that I suspected kidney stones and gave him pain medication. We packed up, drove 500 miles for nine hours to Mexico City with him in pain. At the American-British Hospital an English-speaking doctor diagnosed kidney stones and put him in the hospital for five days with continuous IV's and strained his urine. He did pass a small stone eventually. Amazing how something that small can knock a person out of whack!

Through the years, when we needed dental services, Dr. Buddy Gregory, a friend of our cousins in Houston, did our dental work free of charge. All three of us had work done on our teeth in 1970. Carl had a crown on one tooth and I had a dental bridge. An abscessed tooth required a root canal treatment and Carrie needed a couple of fillings. Thanks to Jack and Shirley Frey's hospitable invitation, we spent two relaxing weeks in their lovely home near Houston, Texas.

R & R Activities

Our stateside friends always asked what we did for recreation and relaxation. On Sundays we usually had a time of Bible reading, prayer and hymn singing with the three of us. Or we walked upstream to a secluded bend in the river for a family outing and cool swim. We spread out a blanket on a big boulder, ate tuna sandwiches with good fresh bread I baked the day before, had tomato wedges and drank lemonade from a canteen.

Some days we saddled up the horse and rode thirty minutes up the hill about a mile and a half out of town. The trail led to a pine forest where the grass was cool and green. To relax in style, we hung our hammocks from the trees! Being away from people's demands for about two hours was refreshing. We breathed in the fragrance of the pine woods, and clear, refreshing air. From the ridge we could look eastward and see the sparkling blue Gulf waters in the distance as the beaches curved gracefully around the Gulf of Mexico. In the other direction we could see our town. You'd never guess a hard day's hike of 25 miles over rugged jungle trail lay between the two. We thoroughly enjoyed those days free of interruptions and loud music.

God's Talk

Often we arranged to meet John and Royce Lind's family for a picnic lunch in this same pasture halfway between their Popoluca town of Ocotal Chico and our Aztec town Mecayapan. We always had lots of good food and wonderful visits. It was such a treat to have someone else to speak to in English. The children built a *champa* (playhouse) and took turns riding the mule and burro through the trees. Carrie liked the horse to jump over fallen logs.

One Sunday morning Carl and Carrie made breakfast for me, complete with cinnamon biscuits, scrambled eggs, orange and coffee. That was a restful day. What a treat to stay in bed an extra half hour. And it wasn't even a holiday!

Townspeople told us about a beautiful waterfall about one and a half hours away by trail. So one day we decided to explore the countryside in that direction. We planned a picnic lunch of tuna sandwiches, hardboiled eggs, cooked beans and bananas. Hipolito, our language helper, accompanied us. Juanita Salas, her nine-year-old sister Maria, and two younger brothers, Elias and Jose went along to keep Carrie company. Then Juanita's mother showed up, too! She brought a basket of fresh made tortillas as their contribution to the lunch. We weren't sure if she wanted to chaperone her 16 year old daughter or if she was just eager to get in on the fun. I have a suspicion the former is nearer the truth. Now instead of six as we had planned, there were nine of us, The three youngest, Elias, Maria and Carrie, were perched on Macho, our faithful mule. We made quite a procession down the trail.

As the morning passed it got quite hot on the trail, and we welcomed each stream we crossed where we could cool off with fresh clear water. About 11:30 a.m. we reached the falls. The gushing water tumbling 300 feet down the cliff truly

Life and Work in Mecayapan, Veracruz, Mexico

We relax in hammocks tied up in the cool pine forest on a Sunday afternoon.

was beautiful, cool and refreshing. There was a big pool of clear water to swim and bathe in. Juanita, Maria and Mama immediately set to work showing us how to gather fresh-water snails, fresh-water shrimp, crabs and small fish to supplement our lunch. The men and boys went down stream to try their luck at spearing fish.

By the time a fire was ready, we each had collected a variety of natural foods from the jungle stream and gathered leaves as big as dinner plates from a plant called *acoyo*. To cook these delicacies, Mama wet each big leaf thoroughly, wrapped the fish, crabs and shrimp in them then tucked each one carefully into the coals for a few minutes to roast. The wet leaves imparted a delicate flavor similar to anise (licorice), making a very tasty meal, leaves and all.

God's Talk

The Salas family liked the lunch we shared with them. They had never eaten tuna sandwiches before. The afternoon was spent fishing, chatting and enjoying the coolness of the tropical vegetation. It was nearly 5:00 p.m. when we got home, tired from the trail trip, but glad for the happy adventure with our Aztec friends. It was an excellent opportunity to practice Nahuatl phrases and learn more about the ways of the people. But the "fun" wasn't over yet, our bodies were loaded with ticks from the trail, too. As we meticulously picked them off one by one, we said it was all worth it.

One very hot day in August we checked into a beach hotel in Coatzacoalcos. The Gulf waters were like a big warm bathtub with a gentle tide lapping at the edges. It was almost unbearably hot and humid so we spent all afternoon at the beach. To cool off further, we ate our fill of ice cream cones at a little place that had the best ice cream we had found – in 10 flavors, too, mind you! Good ice cream was hard to find and not always safe to eat. We all enjoyed ice cream since we didn't have a refrigerator at that time.

That evening on the beach our car battery went dead! We hadn't had any supper, just an ice cream cone. So, while we waited for it to charge, Carrie said she was hungry for shrimp. We found a little restaurant across from the hotel and ordered shrimp salads. Next morning we discovered the generator needed to be replaced. We got that fixed without too much expense. Then we all went for ice cream cones again before leaving for Mecayapan. What a mix of relaxation and fretting about a vehicle malfunction!

In November of 1968, Mom and Dad Minter pulled their travel trailer from Abilene, Kansas, to Mexico City for an extended visit with us over the holidays at the Wycliffe headquarters. Our plan was to take vacation together and visit cousins Howard and Pearl Wolgemuth, Brethren in Christ missionaries in Nicaragua.

After New Year's Day we first went to our village for ten days where they experienced life in a primitive village. They helped us clean up the house, haul drinking water and set up temporary housekeeping as best we could. Curious people came to our house to meet my parents. Mom and Dad were eager to attend the native congregations so we visited each of the meeting-groups: communion service at Luke's group with tortilla pieces and grape Kool-aid, church dedication at the upper group, a baptismal service in the river at the bottom of the hill, another church dedication with a tamale supper served afterwards. We were so pleased that the typewritten copies of Acts which we had left with the leaders were being used in the church services. One of the men said, "What we need is the whole Bible in *Mela' Tajtol*, (The True Language) meaning their heart language, Nahuatl. It was very hard for them to understand the Bible in Spanish.

Both Mom and Dad suffered with open sores on their legs and arms from scratching sand flea bites. In fact, they could hardly sleep because of the intense itching. In spite of all that, they were impressed with life in the village but glad to leave the sand fleas behind!

After we closed up the house and left our car in Acayucan, we drove together in the folks' car towing their travel trailer, crossed the isthmus on the Pan-American Highway to the Pacific Ocean, admired the lush vegetation all along the highway, perspired most of the way in the humidity since the car didn't have air conditioning.

To make a long story short, our travels took us into Guatemala, Honduras, El Salvador and finally Nicaragua. We

God's Talk

saw homeless people and abandoned children sleeping on the sidewalks. Teams of oxen plodded along the road carrying produce of various kinds in rustic wooden carts. We ate lunch by a vast field of sugar cane where we could watch them process the cane juice with a sugar cane press. The workers filled a jar with pure cane syrup for us -- fresh out of the press. Delicious!

We arrived in Managua about 5:00 p.m. What a relief to see familiar faces. Howard and Pearl were so gracious and had several sightseeing trips planned for us. They took us to the beach for a swim and we gathered lots of beautiful, unique sea-shells to bring back home. We will long remember their pet parrot whose shrill, raspy voice woke us early every morning yelling loudly and repeatedly: "Howard!" "Perla!" "Hallelujah!" "Amen!" We got a lot of laughs out of parrot talk.

The Nicaraguan Christians welcomed us warmly as we attended the evening services that were held outside under the trees on make-shift benches, a lively congregation that Howard and Pearl had helped to start several years ago. We left Managua and headed back over the same route to Mexico City, thankful for a safe, memorable journey.

Language Work

Learning the Language

In October 1973 The Mexican government made an official decision to call the language the Aztec people spoke by its original name – **Isthmus Nahuatl**.

Since Isthmus Nahuatl was still an unwritten language, we had no books to study. Instead, we learned vocabulary by listening, listening, and more listening, writing down every piece of data, organizing it in a file, using the scientific skills we had learned in our linguistic training. Over the first two or three years, as we studied and analyzed the sounds and phrases, we finalized the alphabet using the Spanish letters, except for three distinct sounds that weren't in the Spanish language. We chose characters from the International Phonetic Alphabet to symbolize those three sounds in the Nahuatl language.

(Note: All this language data we were gathering formed the basis of the grammatical structure of the Nahuatl language. Carl

God's Talk

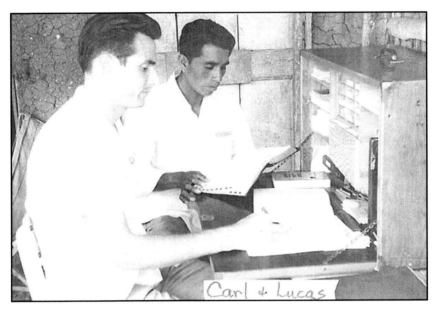

Carl and Lucas work at finding the best way to express the Scriptures in Nahuatl.

---

authored a grammar book in the language that was published in 1980. We both worked on the bilingual Nahuatl-Spanish dictionary that was published in 2002. Both of these books have received wide acceptance among the people and are described near the end of our story.)

Out in the village a big distraction to language learning and translation was the loud, raucous Spanish music that blared from loudspeakers in the two *cantinas* (taverns). It could be heard all over town day or night. They pumped out music so loud we could hardly sleep. If we were tired the next day we were not as eager to learn new words!

We encountered another problem: the people's negative attitude toward their own language. They wanted to learn Spanish, the "prestige" language. They had often been ridiculed by "outsiders" saying their language was only gib-

Language Work

berish and not worth anything. This attitude affected their ideas about translating the Scriptures into their language if it wasn't worth anything. We hoped to kindle a flame of eagerness for them to preserve and continue using their own language in addition to learning Spanish.

We aimed for maximum exposure to the language and used every opportunity to hear conversations. Men gathered at our house after their day's work in the fields and helped Carl with Nahuatl phrases. He had a very good ear for hearing the subtle nuances that were critical to becoming fluent. He spent more time around town and had greater exposure to the language. By offering to help with community projects such as putting a new thatched roof on the pastor's house, he had opportunities to practice the language.

It went a bit slower for me to learn Nahuatl. The women had precious little time to teach me the language since they were busy all day long washing clothes, grinding corn, carrying firewood, making tortillas, tending the babies, or bringing in produce from their fields. I had to be creative if I was going to get language practice so I went along with them sometimes. This was an excellent way to learn not only language but culture, observing ways they did their work and related to each other.

Women and teenage girls willingly gave me words and phrases when they could visit me. And then it was practice, practice, practice! One of us needed to stay home most of the time to greet visitors and give medical care so we took turns visiting in people's homes where we could hear them converse among themselves.

When someone brought me a basket full of unshelled black beans, Carrie and I enjoyed shelling them as we sat on low

God's Talk

stools near the fireplace and listened to the women chat with us around the fire. Wonderful language learning opportunities! I always had a pencil, a stack of 3x5 cards and a notebook handy to write down (and later file alphabetically) words and phrases in context to better grasp the meanings as we studied them later. One day after a visitor left, Carl bounced excitedly into the house exclaiming, "Hey, I just had a conversation in Nahuatl!" Each small sign of progress was cause for rejoicing.

Carl writes:

> *I playfully taught the younger kids a simple English phrase "Oh my achin' back!" They went off into gales of laughter merely by hearing the rhythm. When I explained the meaning of it, they laughed even harder and so did we! They knew all there was to know about aching backs, a common complaint here. No wonder. They stooped to do so many tasks -- laundry on the rocks in the river, patting tortillas on the metate, cutting grass with machetes, chopping and gathering firewood and carry it in large bundles on their backs. One day I was in Soteapan when a kid waved at me and yelled, "Oh my achin' back!" I had an achin' back myself after I had lifted, balanced and lashed two 130-pound butane tanks for our gas stove on to the back of the pack mule. The pack mule must have had an achin' back, I'm sure!*

Learning to Speak Correctly

It is here that I hope you will bear with me while I brag a bit on Carl's expertise in linguistics. He had an extraordinary sense of hearing when it came to discerning the subtle nuances of the language.

Language Work

When the linguists who preceded us, Dr. Howard and Joan Law, were learning the language, neither of them picked up on a very special significant sound that makes the difference between past and present tenses of a verb. Howard told us later that he knew something was there but he couldn't quite pinpoint it or describe it.

At our first linguistic workshop, with the expert consultant help of Dow Robinson, translator in a related Nahuatl dialect, Carl was successful in breaking into that mystery. He called it vowel laryngealization. A brief description goes like this: when a vowel occurs at the end of a verb, it can have one of three sounds that represent which tense it is -- present, past or future. For present tense, this sound consists of a soft glottal stop (a quick catch in the throat, like when we say uh-oh in English) followed by a barely discernible puff of air. This is the sound that tells the listener that something is happening now. For past tense, the sound is a hard glottal stop. For future tense the sound is just a puff of air.

This was an incredible breakthrough! It was a complete turnaround for us to begin Scripture translation so that it would make sense to the native speakers of this language. At the workshop Carl published a scholarly paper about that aspect of the language that has since helped other linguists and Bible Translators.

As for myself, it took me between six months and a year to really be able to reproduce this laryngeal vowel sound correctly in a stream of conversation. Once I grasped it, though, I was then able to speak more fluently.

To practice the language I often visited my next door neighbors in their hut sitting on low stools around the tiny fire on the floor. In my faltering way, I tried to say "My back is

God's Talk

hurting." However, to my chagrin and humiliation, with the simple twist of a consonant cluster, it came out, "My banana is hurting." Great shrieks of laughter all around, they nearly fell off their stools! They never let me forget that one! Such are the pitfalls of language learning. They had great patience with me and when I goofed I learned to laugh along with them. Sometimes it was hard not to get discouraged, though.

I listened carefully when the women conversed together. There were several differences between women's and men's vocabulary -- the men called it "women's talk" and wouldn't be caught dead using those phrases. Juanita's mother and another lady agreed to let me record them conversing. When I played it back for them they laughed hysterically as they listened to themselves talk. This was a new experience for them.

I found out that a "granny knot" in Nahuatl is called a *sihua' ta-ilpil*, a woman knot. Nahuatl is noted for its long words. Example: ***xinetaxcalkimilowili*** means , Wrap it up for me in a tortilla. ***Timokechnawahtiwitzej*** means, We will come arm in arm.

Fluency in the language came slowly but surely for us. We used our tape recorders extensively to record and transcribe text material such as stories, legends, and conversations. Then, with the help of a native speaker, we would play the tape back and write the text out phonetically. It was so frustrating when our battery-operated recorders had spells of not working.

These transcriptions were the basis of language analysis, research and study during a three-month linguistic workshop we attended in September 1966 at the Ixmiquilpan Translation Center 100 miles north of Mexico City. Carl worked

Language Work

steadily on the technical linguistic analysis during the workshop and made good progress describing the phonetics of the language: vowel length, the puff of air at the end of a word and glottal action. It took a long time to figure out the long and short vowels in words that use the same letters.

One example: drawing out one vowel a bit longer makes a difference between beating something or moving it, following a man or burying him! A barely discernible puff of air at the end of a verb indicates that it is plural. The glottal stop at the end of a sentence indicates that it is past tense. For example: One pair of words that gave us trouble was *quipata* vs. *quipaata*. In the first one, the short vowel is written with only one 'a' in the middle and is pronounced very quickly. In the second word, I've written the long vowel with 'aa' in the middle of the word: *quipaata;* the middle 'aa' is drawn out about one second longer. Tricky! *Quipata* means to mix it up; *quipaata* means to put an object in another place. One morning I told Silvia, *"Inimej piotecsis xicpata ipan chiquihui'."* (Mix up these eggs in the basket.) Silvia was puzzled for a moment, then laughed when she figured out my mistake. I had meant to say, *"Inimej piotecsis xicpaata ipan chiquihui'."* (Put these eggs in the basket.) No wonder we had days when we despaired of ever learning to speak fluently.

At the workshop, expert consultants were there to help us analyze the sounds and grammatical structure of the language more fully, a very necessary step to prepare for accurate Scripture translation later on. After all this, we were much more fluent in the language. When we returned to Mecayapan, people glowed with pleasure when we used Nahuatl exclusively and didn't resort to sign language or Spanish like we had to do before. Learning the language was one of the hardest parts of our work, but it really paid off in dividends of friendships, loyalty and the people's genuine

God's Talk

This shows details on one of the thousands of 3" x 5" cards we wrote for every new word we came across

acceptance of us.

Silvia told me most people were pleased that we wanted to learn to talk like they did but others were reluctant to accept that we were there to help them. Some were skeptical and believed we were going to make a lot of money by selling their language when we leave the village. The skepticism diminished as we published literature and taught people to read their own language.

The school children, especially, were fascinated when we began writing their spoken language down on paper. Most of them could read Spanish, so it didn't take them long at all to read Nahuatl because they could understand what they were reading.

It must have seemed remote and foreign though, to those who, until recently, knew little or nothing of what those funny marks on paper meant. The many hours we spent at the desk were not in vain. Their enthusiasm of seeing their language in writing was rewarding to us and them. They began to understand what all those little slips of paper were for that we filed in the big box on the desk. Soon we offered literacy classes to teach the people to read and write their own language

Carl writes:

> *One winter night in January some fellows came around as usual after dark. They were unaware the tape recorder was turned on so they talked freely and naturally. The next day when we transcribed the conversation, we discovered that one fellow had said in Nahuatl (since he figured we wouldn't understand him), "Don't help him, he's not paying you. He will just go and sell our language." When I went over the tape again with Genaro we discovered another fellow suggested giving us nonsense syllables. I never knew what mischief a bunch*

```
F3/1                      5                    m-a-m
Se taga' yajqui que quipiato por la suertej se
gansoj. Entonces inón igansoj pe' tatajcal. Cada
díaj quicahuaya itecsis de puro oroj. Inón itecsis
como de puro oro pues quinamacaya bonitos precios
iga patiyoj. Comati tomin.quitaya quiquixtiaya ipan
inón piotecsis. Cada díaj quicajtoya itecsis inón
gansoj. Pero inón hombrej, yéj amoconvencerohuaya
que porque sejsé quicahuaya itecsis inón gansoj.
Yéj qnxnsqnxxx quinequiaya más. Quinequiaya achi
ejeyi, achi najnahui al díaj maquicá itecsis inón
pobre animal./ Entonces lo que quichi yéj como
amocontentaroj iga sejsé diaroj, major quijtoj yéj
"Anca más bueno manicmicti-pa. Iyijtico an quipia
anca cien o docientos itecsis. Pero maquipia cien,
qué grande cantidad ompa nicpia al jalonazoj, nia
nicnamacati.
```

Here is a bit larger sample of what the language looks like in print. The underlined vowels indicate they are held a bit longer, the single quotation mark indicates a glottal stop. This is an excerpt of the story of "The Goose that Laid Golden Eggs."

of fellows might have in mind when they came around. It was obvious some still distrusted us and were suspicious of our motives. That was just something we had to work around.

Linguistic Analysis and Translation Process

Workshops at Ixmiquilpan

In May 1966, less than a year into our life in the village, we had a big decision to make about who to take with us to our first Literacy Workshop. This three week workshop was designed to teach several native language helpers, who came from different people groups, how to organize and teach reading and writing classes in their own languages back in their villages.

Carl writes:

> *During the years we lived in Mexico, we spent several months at a time at specialized workshops. We brought native language helpers along with us from the village. The Ixmi Center was a wonderful setting for teams to go for intensive study. Each team was assigned one of 12 cubicles in the workshop building. Consultant help was available for linguistic, translation,*

God's Talk

literacy, grammar, dictionary and native-authored literature projects in each language.

It was much easier to concentrate at a place like this, away from the many interruptions of village life. What a pleasant change it was to live in one of the twelve modest but comfortable duplex apartments, with real furniture, kitchen appliances and other amenities such as phone, bathroom and laundry facilities. There was good fellowship, prayer and Bible Study groups with other translators and support personnel.

The small town of Ixmiquilpan (pronounced ish-mee-KEEL-pahn or ISH-mee for short) was a quiet, pastoral, serene place in the high desert 80 miles north of Mexico City - a welcome change away from the hustle and bustle of traffic in the big City. There was a small grocery store and huge weekly produce market downtown. An Otomi woman from the nearby Otomi village came by each apartment daily with freshly-made corn tortillas for sale.

The grocery store was reminiscent of an old-fashioned store, not self-service. Don Carlos stood behind the counter and you told him what you wanted. If you had a choice of flavors, like jello or jam, he invited you to step back into the stock room and make your selection. He weighed out your sugar, flour, and rice. Then he added it all up by hand on a little slip of paper cut from something printed on one side. When I asked him if there was a good place in town to buy tires, he not only told me where to go but he phoned for prices. Personalized service was alive and well in Mexico.

Genaro Gonzales and Lucio Bautista were the two fellows we invited to go with us. Genaro, an intelligent 15-year-old old who could read and write well, was quick to learn. He was willing to repeat words and phrases several times until he was satisfied that we said it right and then wrote it down. His one question was: "Will there be people there that will laugh at me because I'm an Indian?" Carl, realizing his sensitive nature, assured him that nobody would laugh at him. There would be language helpers from ten different people groups and they could be supportive of each other. That seemed to put him at ease.

Lucio, age 22, Genaro's cousin, also agreed to go with us. They were good company for each other and provided both Carl and me with a language helper to work with so we could accomplish that much more. For three solid weeks we worked diligently with the two fellows and learned a lot of language. We took time on weekends to visit places like Chapultepec Castle, and the anthropological museum in Mexico City, and the famous pyramids at Teotihuacan, northeast of the city. Genaro and Lucio were thrilled to learn about their own Aztec history.

September 1966 – Linguistic Workshop

Carl writes:

> *As I read in I Corinthians 13, 14, and 15, I was impressed with the beauty and worth of the Scriptural truth. In these months of learning Nahuatl I pray the Lord will guide us into learning language that will be most useful in translation of the precious Word, and that we won't miss noting and filing important*

God's Talk

things. I see how necessary it is to be deep into the Word during these learning days.

I needed to take care of some government papers in Mexico City before the workshop started. A week later Marilyn and Carrie stayed there while I returned by bus to Acayucan to bring Epifaneo and his daughter Silvia back with me to Ixmi. They had agreed to be our language helpers for the Fall Linguistic Workshop.

In faith, I bought three return bus tickets for the 9:00 p.m. departure. Sure enough, after the tiring all-night bus trip I arrived in Mecayapan. They were ready to go by 4:00 p.m. It had been raining steadily for two nights and a day so the trail was like a river of mud. I walked barefooted because I would have to take off my boots anyway to cross the swollen stream. How I did slide around! Several people going back toward Mecayapan said "Don't try to cross the river! It's rising."

Each translation team was assigned to one of the 12 offices that surrounded a small courtyard. Carl and Epifaneo work on linguistic data.

Linguistic Analysis and Translation Process

Sure enough, when we got to the Huasuntlan river, the current was rushing too fast and too high to cross on foot. By that time it was dark. An hour earlier we could have made it, but after nightfall it looked much too threatening and menacing. The water kept getting higher and deeper so we turned around and returned to the village. Back at the house I fixed us a snack and at midnight, I said, "Let's get some rest and wait till things get a little drier." We washed our muddy feet and went to bed in our clothes. I hated to lose those bus tickets.

Next morning Pablo loaned us his horse and a burro for the baggage. Bless him! We started back over the trail. During the night the water had receded enough to let us cross the river. At the bus station in Acayucan they wouldn't accept the unused tickets. Hmmm, $200 pesos down the drain! Thankfully I had enough money to replace those tickets and be on the first bus scheduled to leave at midnight. We were so relieved to arrive safely at Ixmi after our all-night bus ride.

We helped Epifaneo settle into the language helpers' quarters with other fellows. Silvia's room was in the apartment where we were to live.

Our two main goals were to learn what we could about vowel length and glottal sounds, and work on the bilingual dictionary. Our consultant was Dow Robinson, translator for another dialect of Nahuatl, who gave us excellent ideas for analyzing our dialect. Epifaneo was superb help as we sifted through page after page of text. We wrote up lists of words, made observations, watched for linguistic patterns and recorded a list of four-syllable compound words with all 16 combinations of vowel length patterns. It was a tedious process and we both became brain-weary after several hours of desk work. Frequently Epifaneo and I laughed at my efforts to become more fluent in Nahuatl.

God's Talk

After we had come to some final conclusions about the long and short vowels as well as the very complex patterns of glottal action, I authored an article describing what we had learned. That was published in a linguistic journal. Later I wrote up a ten page text that described Aztec marriage customs and submitted it to an anthropological publication.

One Saturday in October the five of us, Epifaneo, Silvia, Carrie, Carl and I started out early one morning for a relaxing sightseeing day in Mexico City. As we rolled smoothly along on the main highway in our red Ford, suddenly we heard a loud crack and rasping sound--the lower ball joint had broken and slipped out, letting the wheel turn outward and cram itself back up into the wheel well. The right front corner of the car dropped as we screeched and scraped to a halt, sparks and smoke flying! The tire was ripped down to the cord on the bottom edge. Fortunately we were on a straight stretch of highway in the country and could glide to a stop safely by the side of the road.

A truck driver, headed the opposite direction, stopped to offer help. He offered to send a truck to tow us back to the town of Pachuca that we had just passed through. Two hours later the truck arrived and towed us in to Zamora's repair shop. We were told that the part that needed replacing would cost $870 pesos! What could we do but have it replaced? It would take at least two days.

Since it was noontime, Señor Zamora took us to his home where he and his wife graciously showed us the best of Mexican hospitality by serving us a wonderful meal. Then he drove us to the bus station and we returned to Ixmiquilpan, thankful to have avoided a serious accident! We were very grateful for and impressed with his generosity and thoughtfulness. Two days later, we all hopped on a bus

Linguistic Analysis and Translation Process

back to Pachuca again and picked up the car with its new wishbone and ball-joint. We arrived in Mexico City with no further problems and did some sightseeing.

For one of our simple but tasty meals we had beans, Mexican rice, pickled chile peppers and *quilmol* (a spinach-like vegetable). Silvia cooked it, thickened the juice with cornmeal and added tomatoes. For dessert we had popsicles. Epifaneo dipped his fork in the chile pepper juice and sprinkled it on his strawberry popsicle. He said he should have used a little more pepper juice! This fitted in with the "hot" and "cold" theory the Aztec people have. In their way of thinking, cold foods need to be balanced out with something hot and vice versa.

When workshop was over, we headed back to the village which meant adjusting to a primitive lifestyle all over again. That was not as easy as one might think. After being away for several months, we were spoiled with household conveniences such as refrigerator, electricity, phone service, baths in a real bathtub, hot and cold running water, kitchen sink and stove. But, hey, there is a lot to enjoy in the village, too.

Silvia is pictured here with our family on our front porch.

God's Talk

January 1968 - Translation Workshop

Lucas and Virginia.

Lucas, the leader of one of the growing Aztec churches in the village, and his wife Virginia agreed to go with us to the translation workshop. They were expecting their first child and we hoped they would have a smooth adjustment to a drastically different environment. Also, our good friend Silvia, again went with us. By now she was like a big sister to Carrie. It was good, too, for Virginia to have another woman with whom she could speak Nahuatl.

A myriad of details were needed to prepare for an extended stay away from the village. Lucas had to arrange for someone to take care of his *milpa* (corn field) while he was gone and to have enough animals to carry cargo for six people. We were inundated with food gifts as our friends came to tell us goodbye--eggs, beans, squash and a native root called *jicama* whose texture resembles a huge radish, sweet, juicy and delicately flavored. We took it all with us to boost our diet and go easy on our pocketbook since we cooked our own meals at workshop.

While Carl and the men loaded the burros, I walked over to our neighbors, Uncle Nick and his wife. Tearfully he said how much he would miss us. He said he was so grateful for

Linguistic Analysis and Translation Process

how I doctored his leg after he tripped over our shoe scraper. Tears came to my eyes when he called me an endearing term, *notzoyotzin* (my little relative). It was touching to have so many people trust us and take such an interest in us.

The six of us arrived at Ixmi about 9:00 p.m Saturday, a late hour to arrive, but we quickly helped Lucas and Virginia get settled for the night in one of the apartments for language helpers. It was no simple task to transplant someone from a primitive village setting to citified ways and surroundings. We instructed them about how to turn electric lights off and on, open and close doors with knobs and locks, use a flush toilet and how to sleep <u>between</u> the sheets; otherwise they would roll up in the spread like they do at home. But if that's the way they were used to doing it, we had no objection. We just hoped they would be contented and healthy here. There was always the chance of being interrupted by sickness, or restless, discontented, homesick language helpers.

The next day, as I collected kitchen items so Lucas and Virginia could fix their own breakfasts and suppers in their apartment, I saw Silvia and Virginia giggling and whispering between themselves. They told me I was like a mother-in-law setting up housekeeping supplies for a new daughter-in-law in the village. To them this was hilarious.

We all plunged in to work hard on our language projects over the next three months. Silvia, Virginia and I worked on translating Genesis Bible stories into Nahuatl. This would help the believers better understand the New Testament. Both of them had heard some stories in Spanish but understood very little. Luke and Carl worked on linguistic analysis and translation of the Book of Acts. It was beautiful to see how enthusiastic Lucas was about translating the Scriptures into his heart language. We were so grateful for a good spirit of cooperation and adjustment.

Carrie enjoyed having friends her age to play with in the large grassy area. She was right up with the other first grade kids in the school at Ixmi with a volunteer missionary teacher. It was gratifying to know I had done an okay job of using the home-school lessons to teach her.

Carl's work was interrupted when he suffered what we thought at first to be appendicitis, but during surgery the surgeon noticed the appendix was not inflamed. Instead, he diagnosed the severe abdominal pain as a typhoid infection and gave him medication for it. It cleared up immediately. The good news is, he'll never be bothered by appendicitis in the future.

Lucas was able to work with translation on his own for those few days Carl was gone. When Carl went over the verses Lucas had translated he realized how his spelling and translation ability had greatly improved. Translation of Acts went full speed ahead with up to twelve verses completed each day. In the fourth chapter, Lucas was impressed with Peter's bold stand before the authorities.

One evening Silvia went with me to a surprise party for Elaine Beekman at Ruth Anderson's apartment. We had to be very quiet so Elaine wouldn't hear us when she came to the door on a trumped up errand. Silvia said it reminded her of when village people had to hide from the rebels during times of political uprisings in the Aztec area. It was refreshing to see things through her vivid imagination. She interpreted new things in terms of her past experiences.

Even though she couldn't understand the English conversation, she carefully studied the women's facial expressions and analyzed their different laughs. Later she shared her impressions of the laughs and how they sounded to her: one was like a goat bleating; another sounded like a bird that signals bad news when it yells. I had to laugh at her descriptions.

Carl writes:

Valuable consultant assistance was available at the workshop. Also a whole reference library of Bible translation commentaries, versions and back-translations from other Indian languages. Excellent lectures with discussion were given several times a week. Two distinguished guest lecturers shared insights with us--Dr. Bill Wonderley of the American Bible Society and Dr. Dan Fuller of Fuller Theological Seminary.

The extraordinary, personal help by specially trained Wycliffe linguist/translator consultants was most welcome to those of us who struggled to make sense of a new language. They checked the work we and Lucas did verse by verse along with Lucas to be sure he could clearly understand it. Even with consultants and the Lord's help, translation was slow and tedious at this early stage, but we trusted the end result would be clear and meaningful to our people. For example, we looked for the best way to express the idea of being filled with the Holy Spirit, a crucial subject in the book of Acts. Each morning before we began, we asked God to help us express it clearly in Nahuatl. To see Lucas' understanding develop was a special satisfaction. By the end of the three months Lucas and I had translated and

God's Talk

checked the first nine chapters. Acts 9:31 was a good stopping place for now and we published that much in a booklet.

When workshop was over in June, we took Lucas, Virginia and Silvia to the bus station to go back home while we stayed in the City two more weeks. Some relaxing time included a fun day at the famous Xochimilco flower gardens, gliding smoothly down the flower-strewn canals on a boat with singing mariachis to entertain us.

Back in Mecayapan, the humid tropical climate drained the energy right out of us. It was such a drastic change from the warm, dry desert air in Ixmi and the cool, crisp breezes of the high mountains around Mexico City we had enjoyed.

While we were gone, the ten miles of dirt road leading into town from the highway was widened and graded through the jungle. This time it was dry weather so we didn't get hopelessly stuck in the mud with our carry-all like we had many times before. The ominous black, roiling clouds were building up in the north, though, so we knew the rain would soon come down in torrents. After we got home it began to pour and rained 14.2 inches in the next 12 days! We like to think the Lord graciously held back the rain just for us.

We continued checking the rest of Acts with people in the village because a crucial step in getting translated materials ready to publish was to check it for accuracy and clarity with other native speakers who were willing to help Carl for the next several weeks.

Silvia and I continued working on Old Testament stories from Creation through the life of Abraham. After they were published they were received enthusiastically by those who came to listen to the stories each night. The translation workshop in October 1968 had been so helpful in completing other stories--Samuel, David, Daniel, Jonah, etc. The New Testament took on more meaning when people had more Old Testament background.

November 1972 – Native-authored Literature and Creative Writing Workshop

Lazaro, 35 years old, accepted our invitation to go to Ixmi with us for a Native-authored Literature and Creative Writing workshop. His wife and 6 children kept the home fires burning. Lazaro could read and write both Spanish and Nahuatl. He also was a great talker and excellent story-teller. He had a vivid imagination when it came to writing creatively in his own language. Though not yet a believer, he was sympathetic to the Gospel. We prayed he would soon believe God's Talk.

There were 10 native speakers of other languages along with their translators. Writing classes were taught in Spanish by experienced Wycliffe translators. There were also classes in typing, art, music, and field trips to give them experiences on which to creatively express themselves in their own languages. In the art classes they learned to illustrate their own stories, fables, legends and poetry. They enjoyed lots of camaraderie, too.

Lazaro caught on fast to what was expected and was hard at work writing his own impressions of the trip to Ixmi and the big Monday market day. He enjoyed socializing with the language helpers from the other tribal areas and all of them stimulated each other to write more stories. It was fun to see him blossom with his new skill. He wrote several excellent

God's Talk

humorous stories that he knew would stir up people's interest in reading back home.

At the end of the workshop the young authors celebrated with a graduation ceremony and were given certificates to show for their contribution toward literature in their own languages. All this added to their self-esteem. Indigenous people had so often been told by Spanish speakers that theirs wasn't really a language, that they believed it was inferior. Because of this attitude we sensed a reticence to have the Scriptures translated into their language. That changed drastically when they saw it in print!

Back in Mecayapan, we printed booklets of Lazaro's stories for distribution in the village and the people really liked them. As Lazaro shared his fun-to-read stories and cultural legends with people in the village, four more young fellows were inspired to write stories, some several pages long. The school teachers and the children even got into the act by writing and illustrating their own compositions in Nahuatl. Now we had the beginnings of a Nahuatl folklore book which was truly their own!

The story booklets proved to be good preparation for reading Nahuatl Scriptures as fast as we could produce them. They called them *Mela' Tajtohua* (The True Talk) As a result of all this interest in reading, we distributed many more Scripture portions. When people realized their own language was valuable, they had a much greater appreciation for it. How exciting to think these efforts to produce literature that sparked their interest would result in people becoming fluent readers of the Bible. What a blessing it was to see how God provided just the right persons to help us. It gave us more incentive to keep on with the job.

Native-authored stories had another important purpose: they opened the door for us to better understand their culture, beliefs and thought patterns which was so essential to good translation work. As writing caught on in a big way, we were able to understand them even more. It was as if all this time we had just been peeking through the keyhole into their culture.

February 1973 – Dictionary and Grammar Workshop

Genaro and Silvia had married while we were on furlough in 1971. Now they and 11-month-old David agreed to go with us to the linguistic workshop. It was fun to have a baby around the house again starting to do all the things that one year olds do. Carrie enjoyed being "auntie" to David.

Carl and Genaro worked on the Nahuatl grammar, describing it as simply as possible in Spanish, hoping to make it easy for the average Spanish speaker to read. I began analyzing the several thousand words and phrases we had collected and filed in boxes over seven years to be used for the Nahuatl-Spanish dictionary we hoped to publish some day. Experienced consultant help was available at the workshop for both projects which were needed to improve people's attitudes toward their own mother-tongue. It also gave us a sound basis for the ongoing Scripture translation.

We soon became aware that Sylvia was very anemic and needed medical treatment along with more adequate nutrition. Genaro said she had not fully recovered her health from when David was born, wouldn't eat properly and refused to take medicine. One day in our apartment, she had dizzy spells, fainted, had memory loss and incoherent speech. The local doctor admitted her to the small hospital and gave her two blood transfusions to remedy the anemia. After the second transfusion, she reacted to the blood and went into shock. She never fully regained consciousness. It was about 11 o'clock that night when the doctor suggested she be taken to the hospital in Mexico city eighty miles away. Richard Anderson agreed to drive Carl, Genaro and Silvia those two hours to Mexico City. Sylvia died shortly after they arrived. *(Note: In Mexico it is illegal for anyone but authorized persons to transport a corpse. Had she died on the way, they would have been held suspect and jailed until the case was investigated.)*

A quick autopsy showed she had suffered a cerebral hemorrhage. Carl and Genaro, though terribly tired from lack of sleep, spent the next day in government offices working through lots of legal red-tape to permit a hearse to transport her body across state lines and back to the village – a round-trip of over a thousand miles. A Wycliffe friend drove Carl, Genaro and me in his van all night for nine hours to get to the village. *(In Mexico a body is not embalmed and must be buried within 24 hours, thus the need to rush the process.)*

Without telephone service, there was no way we could inform the family in Mecayapan that we were bringing Sylvia's body back. How sad it was for us to meet them in this situation. She was buried that afternoon. Naturally the families were shocked and numbed with grief. Fortunately, they accepted the fact that we had done all we could under the circumstances.

Linguistic Analysis and Translation Process

We gave Genaro a choice--to come back to the workshop with us or remain in the village. We told him that if he chose to continue to help us we would help care for little David. He chose to go back with us. He worried about his future with a small child, elderly parents and uncharitable in-laws. A toddler doesn't thrive well in the village without a mother's care. Returning to Ixmi, he had rough times of deep despondency doubled over with grief. When he would release

Genaro and David shortly after Silvia died.

his pent-up emotions, it drained our emotional energy, too, and we leaned on the Lord for wisdom to comfort him. This experience took its toll on our relationship as well and shattered all of us. Carl, exhausted from stress, sleep deprivation and the frantic pace, was sick in bed several days. I admitted I was tired too. Carrie was good help with David's care--her first experience to take care of a small child.

Back in Mecayapan in July, Genaro and his parents accepted our offer for David to live with us for the next year. A toddler in the house added a whole new dimension to our lives. What a lovable little tyke! I also home-schooled Carrie with seventh grade correspondence lessons that fall. It was a very busy year.

Carl checked the rough draft of the Gospel of Mark with various people in the village. Another prayer answered -- adequate helpers available for this task. Everyone was busy in their fields this time of year but several of the Christian men took turns coming to help us. What a gift! Each time we checked for accuracy and understanding, more people were exposed to the wonderful stories about Jesus! Church leaders at one of the church groups that met every night began to use Nahuatl Scripture reading. We typed up trial copies of Acts 1-9 and distributed them to each leader of the four church groups in Mecayapan as well as others who could read. Three leaders gave favorable responses such as "God's Word really talks the True Talk now." The fourth group didn't respond. We trusted the Holy Spirit would guide them in their understanding.

Enthusiastic believers were meeting nightly and also hiked for several hours by trail to witness to people in other Aztec towns. They reported many gathered for Bible study, sang and listened to the Gospel Recordings in Nahuatl. In one place, four people decided "to believe God's Talk and take God's Trail." We felt the urgency more than ever to get more of the Scriptures in print to nourish the new believers.

Translation Trials

At this point it might be helpful to the reader to understand more about the complexities of the translation and publication process. Once Scripture portions were translated then the really tedious work began. It was typed from the handwritten manuscript, then checked with several native speakers to make sure it was well understood. Lots of changes were made in that process; therefore, it had to be retyped to provide a "clean copy" for the consultant to work with. Check. Check and check some more!! We wished we could get Scripture ready for them faster.

Having an experienced consultant check our work was such a big part of a good translation that it had to be done very carefully and prayerfully. We had to make what was called a back-translation in English since consultants could not understand all the languages. An experienced translator with extra training used a "fine-toothed comb" to check for accuracy and make sure the translated portions conveyed the same meaning as the original. A native speaker reviewed passages the consultant thought needed to be re-worked. Next, a native speaker, who hadn't worked with us before, listened while we read the whole manuscript to check for continuity, clarity of expression and naturalness. The manuscript was checked again, this time for correct punctuation, accents, paragraph breaks, sub-titles, verse numbers and other piddly but important details. After all that, a "clean copy" needed to be typed again to submit for publication. Finally, a staff member in the Mexico City Publication Department keyboarded it on the teletype (an early version of modern computer). Then it could be run through the computer process that was used to speed up the printing of Scripture in the various languages. We needed perseverance to stick to what seemed like an overwhelming job!

We hosted informal Scripture reading groups of people at our home where they felt free to ask questions and make suggestions that would clear up any ambiguous parts. For example, in reviewing Acts 7:30-32 Matias wondered if the angel in the burning bush was the ghost of the Egyptian Moses had killed; their tribal beliefs equated angels with ghosts. Another person understood it to say it was one of Moses' ancestors. It was necessary to specify at the beginning of verse 32, "I am God." Then we went on to say, "I am also the God of your forefathers long ago."

August 1969 - Three-week Scripture Workshop at Ixmi

Two Christian men, Pascual Castillo and Nemorio Revilla, went with us to provide the valuable help we needed to do the final consultant check on Mark's Gospel to insure accuracy and to smooth out some of the rough edges. Pascual was free to come with us because several months before when he was about to throw a "fishbomb" into the water, it exploded in his hand, mutilating it severely. Amputation above the wrist was required, making it impossible to do his field work.

Let me tell you about Nemorio. A year ago Nemi "entered in to God's Way," as the people say it. He told us the hardest for him to give up when he entered in to God's Way were the rowdy fiestas where liquor circulated freely. Fiestas provide their drab lives with short bursts of colorful activity.

But the men became so inebriated, would get into machete fights and did other dreadful things. For someone like Nemorio, who was influential and relatively well-to-do, giving up that life style must have been very difficult. He testified that working with us this time on Mark's Gospel in his own language helped him better understand Christ's life and purpose on earth.

Nemi had obligations at home after the three weeks were over, but Pascual agreed to stay on to read through Mark's Gospel once more before we started it on its way through publication. The World Home Bible League generously provided the funds for publishing, printing and distributing it to the Aztecs a couple of months later. The Creation Story and Old Testament stories of Adam through Abraham were also ready for publication.

Carl writes:

> Excitement ran high among the Christians in the village when published copies of Acts arrived. On November 2, 1968 about 100 members from the four local congregations met together at one of the chapels here in the village to dedicate the newly published portion of Acts in a simple, but very meaningful service in the Nahuatl language. This was an unprecedented occasion for the believers to cooperate like this. From then on the books sold steadily. A school boy came to buy a book at 6:15 one morning. One young man remarked about the attractive cover design: "The cover is beautiful but what's inside is even more beautiful!" His words were music to our ears!
>
> It was a dramatic testimony to unbelievers who were observing traditional rituals for "All Saints' Day" (Halloween) by taking food and flowers to the graves in the cemetery and chanting to appease the spirits of the dead. Later that day, several of our

God's Talk

> *Aztec brethren went with me as we drove 60 miles to Sayula where another Wycliffe team, Larry and Nancy Clark and the Sayula Popoluca people group, were dedicating their completed New Testament, an experience enjoyed by all. The Mecayapan group eagerly expressed anticipation for the day when the Isthmus Nahuatl New Testament would be dedicated.*

In the spring of 1970, Fabian and Genaro came two or three days a week to work on translation. Genaro felt God wanted him to work for Him. Looked like God had prepared **two** for this task! Fabian reported a dream he had--he and Carl were on the trail together "gathering souls."

Working with two people at a time went well. They stimulated each other's ideas and didn't get sleepy like Lucas did. They spent long hours each day at the translation desk to finish the remainder of Acts, then did Romans, II Thessalonians, I Peter, Timothy and Titus letters. The Gospel of Mark and a first draft of the epistles of John, and Jude had been translated earlier.

Carl and the guys first thought Romans would be an easy book, but it turned out to be more difficult and went slower. St. Paul's long and involved sentences were difficult to translate, but good commentaries and several English and Spanish versions of the Bible helped make the job easier. The Spanish versions were often completely over their heads, so when Carl checked to see how they understood the Spanish, it was often exactly the <u>opposite</u> meaning. Then they looked for the best ways of saying it in Nahuatl. Sometimes a whole morning was spent on one or two difficult verses. Often they said, "I never knew it said **that** before!" It was encouraging to see their enthusiasm. After a translation consultant

Linguistic Analysis and Translation Process

checked Romans, it was ready to thread its way through the complicated computerized system and on to the presses.

A phenomenal interest for using the Nahuatl Scriptures in the churches was growing. The freshly translated literature and 2,000 Scripture calendars fresh off the press gave us a good reason to get out on the trails to distribute them to the 30,000+ people throughout the 21 villages. They proudly displayed their calendars in their humble huts.

An organization called Scriptures Unlimited provided tape players and tapes free of charge, and we supplied the batteries when needed. We kept five tape-players out on loan in the homes most of the time. These were also carried to other towns where a Christian witness was just beginning.

Carl made a new set of Scripture tapes, using Nahuatl songs interspersed with several chapters of the recently published book of Romans. At each step of progress, more of our Aztec friends talked eagerly about the day when the whole New Testament will be in their language. We shared their excitement!

How soon could we hope to deliver the whole New Testament to the Aztecs of the Isthmus? Through teamwork, Wycliffe technicians were developing computers to speed up better translations. John Beekman, chief translation consultant for SIL in Mexico and translator for the Chol New Testament, predicted that with the new technology, five years would be a realistic goal for us.

God's Talk

Translation Treasures

Carl realized he had missed putting length on a vowel. It came out, "I will cause your sins to swarm around you." Instead, it should have said, "I will throw away your sins." He quickly saw his error, and changed it to the appropriate word. The figures of speech such as "spiritual milk" and "living stones" were hard to translate. Translation was tricky!

When we came to the part where it says, "Don't refuse anyone that wants to borrow something" I learned a new word that translates: "Don't throw your face away from someone and not give them what they want."

The summer of 1972, Chencho and I worked on Matthew's Gospel. Some parts were amazingly difficult to translate, such as where Jesus said, "Unless your righteousness is better than the Pharisees and teachers of the Law you won't enter God's Kingdom." Chencho wanted to say it in Nahuatl like this, "Unless you are good like the Pharisees and teachers of the law you won't get to God's Kingdom." It was obvious he hadn't grasped the grammatical structure of the Spanish version and also needed more background on how corrupt the temple leaders were. It took a whole afternoon to discuss these two verses until I was satisfied that he understood the true meaning.

The first verses of I Peter chapter three took quite a bit of work to come out clearly. At first Fabian thought it literally was a command for women not to braid their hair or wear clothes! Finally he caught the idea that it was not **just** those things that women were to place emphasis on, but it was the inner spirit that counted the most.

Translation Work in Pajapan

Pajapan was a large Aztec town located about 25 miles east of Mecayapan, along the coast of the Gulf of Mexico. It was possible, but very difficult, to drive there in a 4WD vehicle over a rutty one-lane road across the mountains. The Pajapeños spoke an unwritten dialect of Nahuatl that was closely related to the Isthmus dialect but there were significant vocabulary and grammatical changes, so many that they could not understand each other's conversations.

In 1968, when they saw how Mecayapeños were enjoying their written Scripture, they began to ask for their own translation of Scriptures. One Saturday Carl set out to deliver a set of Gospel records and calendars and get acquainted with the believers there, but it rained. Two of the fellows couldn't go along at the last minute. Carl felt sick when he got up that morning. So that project was temporarily set aside.

When we returned from furlough, believers in Pajapan asked again if we could make the necessary linguistic changes in the translation so it would serve them, too. This was in our long-range plan so it was encouraging to see a genuine flourishing interest.

The World Home Bible League informed us in October 1973 that the Zuidema family in Minnesota had committed to underwrite the entire cost of publishing the Pajapan version of the Gospel of Mark. Now it was important to find the right person(s) to work with us. January 9, 1974 Carl drove the rough gravel road to Pajapan and spent a week helping several of the brethren do some exploratory work on the first five chapters of Mark's Gospel.

God's Talk

Carl and Fabian made some minor changes in Mark's Gospel in the Mecayapan dialect so the Pajapan Christians could have an improved version to refer to. Fabian was very alert to the fine points and sensitive to the differences between the two languages. He had a good sense of which passages needed to be smoothed out.

The Pajapan translation took longer than planned because there were more linguistic differences between the two dialects than was first thought. The grammar was similar but the Pajapeños expressed many ideas differently. Carl drove back and forth for several weeks to work with the brethren. They did not want to accept money in return, either, which was an indication of how hungry they were to have God's Word in their language! The Pajapan version of Mark's Gospel was published in 1980.

When Carrie and I went along with Carl for one week, we "camped" in a vacant thatched-roof Indian hut, cooked our simple meals over an open fire, slept in our Yucatan-style hammocks, washed clothes in the river, ate lots of fresh, warm, tender tortillas and *pan dulce* (sweet bread). There was absolutely nothing that tasted better than the delicious Pajapan bread the local baker baked in his large mud-plaster oven using hot coals.

Literacy Work

Nahuatl is an aboriginal language, totally unrelated to Spanish. It was only an oral language with no written alphabet and no books or other literature to help us learn the language. After we finalized the alphabet, we prepared primers and story books to capture their interest. Literacy was an important part of our ministry. What good would it do to trans-

Linguistic Analysis and Translation Process

late the Bible if they couldn't read it? The young people who attended the school learned to read Spanish in school and they easily switched to the Nahuatl alphabet. Others needed more coaching in order to pick up the subtle differences in the written language. Their faces brightened as they realized for the first time, they **could** read their own language!

My first student was Josefa, our shy, teen-age neighbor. She caught on quickly, and her eyes would light up when she mastered a cluster of syllables as if to say, I can really read; maybe I'm not so dumb after all. By the end of the lesson other eager children were drinking it all in. Their brown eyes sparkled when they recited the syllables they'd learned. If I was called away to treat a sick person, stir the beans on the stove or poke down the bread dough, they went ahead and helped each other. Their enthusiasm amazed me since they

Marilyn and Josefa are joined by a young lady eager to learn to read.

had never before opened a book or been exposed to a written language.

We brainstormed ideas and incentives for learning to read. A large blackboard and bulletin board were added to our front porch area where our visitors came any time of day. We offered occasional prizes; a lending library and book display created a center of interest; magazine pictures were pasted in a scrapbook with Nahuatl captions underneath. I offered snacks: popcorn, cookies, fresh-baked banana cake, coffee. Who knows, maybe they kept coming because they liked the goodies!

Men who came in from their fields in the evenings wanted to read, too. Eager, lively groups of all ages loved to sit and visit by our little fireplace on cool evenings. What priceless opportunities these were to share conversation informally about spiritual things and discuss current topics of village life, such as how to get a pure water supply into a town of this size.

The first edition of 300 attractive Scripture calendars came off the press in 1966. Simple verses could give the people an appreciation of their language and draw them to the Savior. The eagerness people had for them was thrilling. School children came to our house to show off their ability to read the Bible verses. We rewarded them with a calendar to carry home, read to the family and hang in their huts. Even the poorest family could have one. Usually only those rich enough to buy things from merchants in the market towns had a calendar in their house.

Linguistic Analysis and Translation Process

Carl writes:

Recently I mimeographed 100 copies of ten Spanish hymns, including an introduction in Nahuatl. These proved to be the most popular piece of literature. There was a strong, positive response to the hymns. Soon I made another 100 copies. Listening to the music, people practiced reading the printed words that went along with it. They loved to sing, and it was also a powerful witness to their friends and family. Altogether, we printed and gave away 300 copies.

Language Associates

Many people were willing to help us learn the language, analyze the complexity of the intricate grammatical structure and translate Scripture portions. They deserve to be acknowledged in a special way in this memoir. The following vignettes are of those with whom we have worked most closely through the years. Each one had unique and difficult challenges to face, but their readiness to patiently teach us their language was truly a gift. The resulting friendships we formed are priceless.

Hipolito

Hipolito was the first person who offered to work with Carl soon after we arrived. He came to the house faithfully for several months and gave us good language practice. He testified to a change in his life when he believed the Gospel but he said his wife, not yet a believer, made it hard for him to keep a true witness. We were really sorry he used that as an excuse. Hipolito yielded to temptation to go to fiestas, where liquor flowed freely, and bought *aguardiente* ("fire water"-- strong liquor). At first he seemed repentant of his waywardness, but when he got drunk again and didn't come to work the next day, Carl finally told him it wasn't wise for him to continue to work with us.

Juanita

I had high hopes for 16-year-old Juanita. Her father was Chencho, the pastor of one of the groups. She was of marriageable age, could read and write and seemed more mature than the average Aztec girl. She and I worked together on a health booklet and posters. I also taught her to give first aid and to administer certain medicines in my absence. Girls in the village didn't take on responsibility like that, but she was a competent young lady.

While we were away at a workshop, she married Adrian, an unbeliever. His father owned a beer joint in the village. With the scarcity of Christian young men, what was a girl expected to do? According to the story we heard, a short time later, another woman claimed she was carrying Adrian's child. He admitted to being unfaithful and took the other woman in, too! Juanita beat him with a stick and threatened to leave him, a rather unusual thing for an Aztec woman to do. Maybe having a bit more education gave her courage to be assertive? I was unsure of the best way to encourage her to keep her faith. Later we were told she was pregnant and living in her parents' home. I wondered what kind of life she would have and who would take care of her and her child. I was limited in how much I could help in this situation.

Silvia

Silvia was in her late teens when she became my most valuable teacher. Through her friendship I gained a greater understanding and appreciation for the village women. She taught me language. I taught her to knit. She cooked and ground the corn for tortillas, patted the tortillas for us to eat with our beans or soup on the *metate* (grinding stone), helped me with the housework and explained customs and cultural incidents as they came up. I listened and took notes as she chatted with other women and when she and Carrie played together. Three times she went with us to workshops at Ixmi. She frequently stayed at our house in the village even though her family lived close by. She preferred to stay with us, she said, because she couldn't sleep well at home due to the bedbugs, rats and crying siblings. It was hard for her to stay awake during our language study. Her quiet, steady friendship was a great blessing to our family.

Genaro

Soon after we arrived in Mecayapan, fifteen-year-old Genaro came around frequently to chat. He was a very pleasant, intellectually bright young man with a winning smile. Great potential! He had been recently baptized and his sincere love for the Lord was a joy to watch.

He had family troubles and was confused about whether to quit school and please his elderly father by helping him in the *milpa* (cornfield). Both of his parents had children from previous marriages, and Genaro was a lonely, only child in this marriage. He was a very unsettled young man but testified to a desire to follow the Lord.

God's Talk

Genaro, Silvia and David

Genaro and Silvia were married while we were on furlough and both continued to follow the Lord. In fact, Genaro seemed to be more settled in his faith and had a strong desire to study more of the Word. He demonstrated some leadership qualities that we hoped he would use to teach others. Soon Genaro and Silvia had a darling baby boy they named David.

As I indicated earlier, tragically, Silvia died while they were with us at the spring linguistic workshop. After her death we took care of one-year-old David. Genaro decided he wanted to attend the Mexican Evangelistic Institute in Mexico City. We paid his expenses for tuition and spending money. He was a part-time student there while he finished up his elementary education in a public night school. He still had times of despondency but said he wanted to work with us to complete the New Testament. We prayed that he would find a Christian companion who would also love his little boy. As time went on though, he became discouraged, moody and disillusioned.

After the linguistic workshop, we had returned to Mecayapan with a toddler in the house! He added a whole new dimension to our lives. What a lovable tyke--an active little boy who enjoyed getting into drawers and cupboards. With the family's permission, David lived with us for sixteen months while Genaro was in school. He learned to feed himself, "go potty," and he babbled almost constantly, most of it in English. We made sure he learned Nahuatl too. Of the three languages he heard, (Nahuatl, English and Spanish) English predominated in his constant chatter. Naturally we got attached to him, but we knew that eventually he would go back with his family. When we left for the States, Genaro's older half-sister and her husband, who had no children of their own, took David, now three, into their care. Our feelings were mixed--sad to leave David but glad that he had a family that wanted him.

Lucio

Carl writes:

> *Lucio was my second language helper. When we read Scripture he came up with the idea promoted by one of the church groups --"Jesus had no father." I often became impatient with how some people interpreted Scripture. When we read chapters of I Peter, Lucio said, "What good does it do me to be able to read and understand the Scriptures if I can't live up to it?" Good question.*
>
> *He had gotten a job in Mexico City as a mechanic and surprised us one day with a short visit, looking like a city boy with his white shirt, tie, dark suit, and well- shined shoes! We were delighted when he told us he continued to walk with the Lord and participated in a church near where he worked. He asked for a copy of some Scripture in Nahuatl and Spanish. That was a good sign he was proud to show people what his language looks like in writing.*

Epifaneo

Carl also writes observations of Epifaneo:

> *Silvia's father, Epifaneo, who helped us so much at the linguistic workshop, had brought only one pair of socks with him. He wore them constantly until they smelled like a dead animal. I talked with him about changing his socks and gave him money*

God's Talk

> *to buy five more pairs. I told him what the dean of men had told me in the college dorm: Change everyday!*

Lucas and Virginia

Luke was a pastor at one of the chapels in Mecayapan and was sensitive to God's leading in his life. He caught on to the translation process quickly and was very helpful. Virginia had a pronounced staccato speech, was more monolingual, used more of the women's talk and knew very little Spanish. I taught her how to knit a sweater when her new baby was due.

Medical Work

In 1965 when we settled in the remote Aztec town of Mecayapan, the *municipio* (county seat) was the largest of several Aztec towns. At that time the town had a census of 4,000 – 5,000 people. It was hard to know exactly how many people lived in other towns because they were widely scattered, tucked far back in the mountains in the state of Veracruz. It was estimated that there were between 30,000 and 40,000 speakers of the Isthmus variety of Nahuatl which covered a large area laced with rugged jungle trails. Only one rough, dirt road into our town was passable by beer trucks in dry weather; there were no cars, telephones or TV. A few people had radios and could hear Spanish programs.

We were at least 50 miles from a doctor with adequate medical facilities. I knew I would be the only doctor, nurse, dentist, and health teacher for miles around. The average yearly income for the indigenous people at that time was around $600 so any medical care they needed had to be affordable for them.

God's Talk

To prepare for the onslaught of sick people that would come, I stocked up on first aid supplies, syringes/needles, suturing materials, a few basic dental tools and a wide variety of medicines including narcotics for pain, antibiotics and remedies for various tropical diseases. These were all available <u>without</u> prescription in pharmacies all over Mexico. We used our own personal funds to buy medicines at a substantial discount and charged the people a minimal amount, if at all. There were times when I accepted produce for payment, and felt humbled when, out of their poverty, they brought us gifts of appreciation--eggs, tortillas, papaya, bananas, a bowl of beans. In God's sight the spirit behind the gift was the important part.

Soon after we arrived, word spread quickly that "the gringos" had medicine. Villagers began coming for treatment the first week we were there. I was frustrated and hampered by not being fluent in the language. Gradually, as I listened carefully and used skills learned in our linguistic training, I became more fluent. By the second year, I could easily explain to the people why, when, where and how they get these sicknesses and how to take the medicine. To be of any significant value, pills for amebic dysentery and other parasitic infections were to be taken for 10 days, but they only wanted to buy one day's dose at a time, maybe two at the most. Almost never could I get them to buy enough for a whole treatment regime. Cost was definitely a factor, of course.

My main working principle was to keep the medical work as simple as possible since, at intervals, we would be away attending workshops for several months at a time. If I could find two or three people that I could teach how to administer first aid, simple treatments and medicines, in my absence that would be helpful. This actually worked out well when

Medical Work

two young men and a young woman came regularly for instruction and demonstrations.

One young fellow came from another village for my "crash course" in how to diagnose the common ailments, prescribe basic medication, give vitamin injections and administer first aid treatment for injuries. He was able to help me when a boy was brought in with a severe head laceration that needed several stitches. The next day the boy's father brought us an egg to express his appreciation, a special gift because eggs were scarce. First Aid was an important part of our ministry.

Next to our language study and translation work, the medical work took most of my time and was the largest part of our ministry. We were on call 24/7. The medical ministry opened the way for a spiritual ministry with many wonderful opportunities to pray with people in their homes at times of crisis.

Our front porch served as a "clinic" and packing boxes made good medicine shelves. We would have liked to establish regular "clinic hours" for dispensing medicine but we never could come up with a schedule. The people didn't know about such things as office hours. That was not what we were there for anyway. We came to provide a service, fit into their way of life as much as possible and not force them to fit into ours. Time was of little value in this culture. They were not usually in a big hurry. Often they waited too long to come in the first place--a few more minutes wouldn't hurt them. Most of the people were early-risers because they walked long distances to their fields. By 7:15 in the morning, I had often dispensed medicine to six or more people. I could expect some to come for medical care at mealtime, but they didn't mind waiting till we were finished.

God's Talk

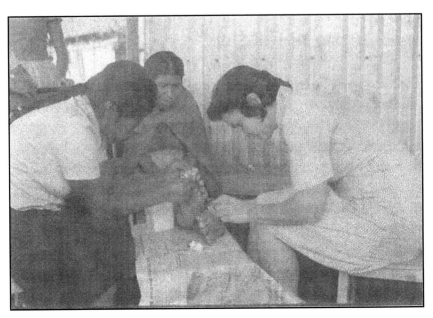

Silvia and Marilyn treat a flea egg infestation for an elderly woman on the front porch.

We referred the most severe medical cases to a newly graduated Mexican doctor assigned by the government to the small, minimally equipped, rural clinic in Soteapan several miles away over the mountain trail. He was expected to spend a year of rural service to pay back his medical school expenses. He spoke only Spanish, however, and it took a lot of persuasion for the Aztec people to go to him since they couldn't understand each other. Sometimes one of us went along to interpret.

The following examples are typical of the type of medical services we provided. There were many I could have included, but time and space do not permit. I had a number of suturing jobs.

One of the first ones was sewing a drunk man's ear back on that was nearly severed from his scalp. The only light I had was the kerosene lamp, so Carl held the flashlight for me. The guy was inebriated enough that he didn't feel a thing. Amazingly it healed nicely.

Another was when an old man's wife bopped him over the head with a piece of firewood during an argument, and gave him quite a gash that took several stitches.

An older boy carried his eight-year-old brother to our door. He had a very deep machete cut right above the knee, severing the tendon. I cleansed it with hydrogen peroxide and closed the wound as best I could, bandaged and splinted it, emphasizing that, if the boy was to ever walk again, they needed to take him to the doctor in Soteapan to have it sutured better than I could do it. We offered our mule for them to use. He took my advice, hoisted the little fellow up and climbed on with him. About 9:00 p.m. they came back with two notes from the doctor, whom we hadn't met yet. On one note he wrote instructions on how to care for the sutured wound, and the other note was a very gracious compliment on our knowledge of first-aid! The boy healed nicely without any complications and eventually recovered the full use of his leg.

One day Carl went to town for supplies and didn't arrive home until after dark. I was all alone when late in the afternoon a man with four fingers nearly severed from his left hand by a machete was brought by his family. It was an ugly, gaping wound with bones and tendons severed. I've seen lots of blood and gore before but never quite like this. It would take more equipment than I had to treat such a severe wound so I cleaned it, wrapped it the best I could and strongly urged them to take him immediately to the doctor in Soteapan. Since it was late in the afternoon, they didn't want to hike the three miles on the trail after dark. They took

God's Talk

him back home again.

Later, Carl hardly had time to climb down off the horse before the mother and sister were at our door asking him to go see the man. They probably thought Carl could do a better job than I did. Not having eaten all day, he quickly grabbed a tortilla, spread it with peanut butter and downed a glass of milk while I fixed the medical kit. He took one of our two-way radios with him. He called back for advice saying they had taken the bandage off and plastered the wound with a black, sticky substance--their native remedy, finely ground-up burnt leather, supposedly to stop the bleeding! Ugh!

Carl cleaned out the gunk, bandaged it again the best he could and gave him a penicillin injection. Before we sat down to breakfast the next morning, a family member asked Carl to re-bandage the fellow's hand because it was still oozing blood. They had taken the bandage off and smeared more burned leather on it! We finally convinced them to take him to the doctor if his hand was ever going to heal. They were from another town so we never did find out if it healed properly. I can't imagine how he ever had full use of that hand again.

Children were brought to me with infected eyes crawling with gnats and oozing with pus. Fever, diarrhea, enlarged abdomens due to intestinal worms, amebic infestation, diarrhea and malnutrition were common. It wasn't unusual to see a child with an abdomen three times the normal size. Little boys' distended bellies were more noticeable since the custom was for boys up to seven years old to run around naked, even in the coldest weather. We kept a supply of a nutritious diet supplement on hand that proved to be just what sick and poorly nourished people needed who were riddled with parasites that sapped the nutrients in their diet.

Medical Work

When village visitors came to see us, they thought nothing of spitting on our rough concrete floor since they did it on their dirt floors at home all the time. I could hardly stand it, though. How do I begin to teach people who haven't the vaguest notion about germ theory? If I had had a microscope maybe they could learn about germs. As it was, my germ theory made no more sense to them than their "bad spirits" or "hot and cold" theories did to me! When they have a "hot" sickness they ask for "cold" medicine. If they have a "cold" sickness they ask if this medicine is "hot." I never could establish a consistent description of which diseases are hot and which are cold. I discovered this is a common belief throughout Mexico, not just in this group of indigenous people. Until I got to know them better I just had to get used to it.

They lived so close to the earth that it was not surprising that lacerations and dog bites became severely infected. Most patients were pleasantly surprised when antibiotics, sutures and clean dressings resulted in quick healing.

One family found transportation to the hospital 40 miles away for their eight-year-old boy who had severely lacerated his foot with a machete. The doctor sutured it and put on a partial cast. A month later the family asked me to check it out. It smelled terrible after not being changed for a month. We helped them get to the doctor for a check-up, removal of the cast and cleaning the wound that had become infected.

An early morning visitor asked if I would go see a sick lady at a ranch 45 minutes one way on a very sloppy, muddy trail. I saddled up the mule and grabbed my bag of medical supplies. Carrie rode along with me this time. The sun was shining brightly when we started out, but by noon a big storm was brewing. The lady was in acute respiratory

God's Talk

distress so there was very little I could do. I gave her what medicine I had, hoping she would get relief. I never got back to that town to see how she got along. Thankfully we were home before rain came down in typical tropical torrents!

Dentistry was not my favorite occupation. I would only pull a tooth if it was already <u>very</u> loose. About halfway through our family devotions one Sunday morning a lady came to have a loose tooth pulled. It took me about five minutes to pull it for her right then and there. Now where else does a tooth get pulled in the middle of Sunday worship service? Late one evening a withered, elderly lady came with aching teeth. I had only one kerosene lamp for light--not the easiest way to pull teeth. I pulled the one tooth that was ready to fall out, applied oil of cloves in several cavities and gave her pain pills. Poor lady, at least 4 more needed to be pulled. But that would come later.

One of the brethren who was a barber asked Carl to pull his tooth. It came out quite easily. When he asked how much he owed, Carl replied, "If you will cut my hair, we'll call it even." How's that for a swap?

One day while I was doing the dinner dishes three children came to the door shyly, covering their mouths with their hands and giggling nervously. Their request was the usual, "Do you have an injection for my brother?" Well, I had no luck finding out what was wrong with the brother, only that he was dying. I didn't know whether to take them seriously. People here will say "I'm dying" or "he's dying" even if they have a sniffly nose! However, I said I would go with them and see what kind of medicine he needed. (Too bad I don't have an injection to cure everything. Some people thought I did.)

Medical Work

As I walked over the ridge and approached the hut where the sick child was, I heard wailing so I knew it was already too late. The two and a half year-old boy had just died. The mother was sitting on the floor holding his limp body close to her chest. She said he had eaten a combination of a tropical root and a green banana then started vomiting and became weaker and weaker, a clear-cut case of the poisonous yucca root. Since there was nothing more I could do for him, I went back home. Five minutes later the children were back again saying another one was dying! This time Carl and Carrie went with me. Sure enough, the four-year-old girl had started vomiting and was in a semi-conscious state. She and two older brothers had eaten the same root. The desperate mother followed our directions to make her vomit, force a strong laxative and offer a lot of liquids. The brothers were older and bigger so the poison didn't affect them quite as severely, but we treated them, too.

At 10:00 p.m. Carl checked on them again and the girl was sleeping quite naturally. In the morning, she was up walking around and the boys were all right, too. At times like this we knew we had to lean heavily on the Lord's strength and wisdom. Our desire was to show His love to all we met.

A mother brought her very undernourished six-month-old baby girl weighing no more than five pounds. I suggested she supplement breast milk with oatmeal gruel and cooked egg yolk. She looked at me aghast, as if I had suggested she kill her! In this culture, babies don't get solid food until they are over one year old. This baby might die too, like lots of others do. Here it is the survival of the fittest.

A five-year-old girl came with a grain of corn lodged in her middle ear, dropped there by a rat running on the rafters above her while she was sleeping. It had begun to swell and was very painful. I reached in with a hemostat (a surgical clamp) and pulled it out. Oh that the remedies were all that easy!

I was called out of bed at 10:30 one night to help a lady in labor with her first baby. She gave birth to a little girl who was born with six fingers on each hand! The sixth "finger", complete with fingernail, dangled beside each of her pinkies, attached only by a small piece of skin. At the request of the grandmother, I amputated both fingers with my surgical scissors. Fortunately, no bones were involved. It pleased them all immensely when I was able to accomplish that. I felt really strange cutting two fingers off of a baby less than an hour old! Healing was prompt and uncomplicated.

One dark and stormy night, after we had gone to bed, a father brought his eight-year-old son who had fallen from the notched pole ladder in his house. His upper teeth had punctured his lower lip leaving a hole about an inch long that was bleeding profusely. What commotion there was! His mother and sisters were wailing and crying hysterically. These people are anything but stoical!

Two of the school teachers came over to see what the excitement was about. The boy, one of their pupils, was stretched out on the table on our front porch. This time I had <u>two</u> kerosene lamps and a flashlight for the operation. He was so tense and scared. I gave him an injection of Dramamine for mild sedation but he needed anesthesia so he would let me come near him with the suturing needle. Carl sprayed ethyl chloride on his handkerchief and held lightly it over the boy's nose. He fought that too at first, but it quieted him enough so I could stitch the lip that was already beginning to swell. Although he squirmed with each stitch, he was sedated enough so that I could quickly put three stitches in his

Medical Work

lip. By the time I finished, his lip looked much better. (Note: ethyl chloride fumes serve as an anesthetic but it is primarily used to treat snake bites by "freezing" the area and decreasing the circulation of the venom.) About half-way through the procedure, I discovered that by dressing so hurriedly in the dark, I had put my dress on inside out and backwards! I decided it made a better scrub gown that way!

One of my helpers worked with me to make health posters and display them in prominent places. My goal was to keep them simple so that cleanliness in this culture would not be an impossible goal to achieve. Making the posters often got pushed aside. I asked myself was I reluctant to begin an educational campaign that would disturb their blissful ignorance? Is it better to be sadly aware or blissfully ignorant? As it was, since they lived so close to the pigs, chickens and dogs that were infested with germs, there was very little they could do to improve sanitation and prevent infestation of parasites.

The posters included five basic ways they could improve health and prevent illness.

- Wash hands frequently with soap (if they could afford to buy it).
- Boil drinking water for ten minutes. (The down-side is it required lots of precious scarce firewood).
- Keep animals away from the eating and sleeping areas (Build a fence).
- Don't spit in public.
- Cook all meat thoroughly.

As I gained fluency in the language, medical work and health teaching took more of my time. It was gratifying

God's Talk

when some people took my teaching seriously. At least two families took the initiative to build adobe-based fire tables and raised their cooking fires up off the dirt floor.

Late one dark, rainy evening, when one of our neighbors came to buy twine, he slipped and tripped over our shoe-scraper, cutting his leg very badly. It was a jagged laceration so it was a challenge to stitch it. We didn't charge him anything and he was so grateful. Later his wife brought us some delicious, hot tortillas that we thoroughly enjoyed! I still miss those soft, tender, dinner-plate-size tortillas that are so lovingly made by hand and taste so good with black beans and chicken soup.

During the winter months we saw severe cases of dysentery, fever and vomiting in babies aged six to eighteen months old. If their parents waited too long to bring them in or they were in poor nutritional condition, they died within 24 hours. If they were brought at the early onset, they did much better. I instructed the mothers how to prepare a salt-sugar-water solution to re-hydrate the child and replace depleted electrolytes.

During the year we were on furlough in 1971, the government helped the townspeople build a modest clinic building in the town square, and a doctor was assigned here. It was great to have a reliable doctor in town. But people are fickle; they didn't want to go to a doctor who didn't speak their language. I was torn between wanting to help the people get the medical care they needed but yet didn't want to compete with the Mexican doctor. They preferred to come to me because I understood their language, and the women and children were embarrassed to talk to a man. Also, he charged higher prices for his services. I often went with them to interpret, or I sent a note in Spanish with them. We

Medical Work

invited him to dinner and he asked lots of questions about what we do there. Before he left he asked for a Spanish Bible. We prayed his interest in the Word would grow.

Twelve-year-old Elodia was born with a severe hare-lip/cleft palate. It was amazing that she survived infancy. A baby born in the village with this problem usually died within a few days because of being unable to nurse properly. We contacted a plastic surgeon in Mexico City, and her mother consented for us to take her to him. He was a Christian and very graciously agreed to operate on her free of charge. He said missionaries had helped him get his education so this was his way of caring for others! Her brother Bennie went along with us so she would feel less homesick. The surgeries went well and she liked her new look! She could eat so much better, too. Her parents couldn't afford all this, so we personally used our meager resources to pay her hospital expenses. Her family was so appreciative of what we did for her. Who knows what God had in store for this young person?

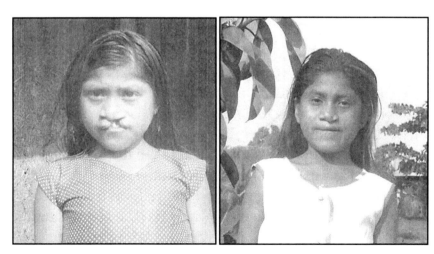

Elodia before and after her surgery to correct her cleft palate

God's Talk

(Ed. note: Twenty three years later in 1997, Carrie, her husband and five children traveled with us to Mecayapan so Carrie could show her family where she grew up. One of the first persons to greet us was Elodia who came to show us her two little grandchildren and bring us a basket full of sweet, juicy oranges!)

We were about to crawl into bed one night at 10:00 p.m. when someone came running to tell us that some people were dying. The whole community was in an uproar. Several members of one family had eaten poisoned rice. We hurried over there but weren't able to do much except make them vomit. Since our carry-all was the only vehicle in town, Carl agreed to take three of the sickest to the hospital in Minatitlan 45 miles away and send an ambulance to get the rest. One and a half hours later, the ambulance arrived, took the old man and his wife who were very near death and two others who were in various stages of convulsions or were unconscious. The old man and his wife died at the hospital. The others survived after they had their stomachs pumped and IV fluids given. Four dogs died after eating the leftovers. Carl didn't get back until 4:30 a.m.

Did someone inadvertently buy the tainted rice at one of the stores in the market town on the highway? A young fellow soon confessed he had stolen it from the ranch where he worked. He didn't know it was laced with rat poison, ready to be scattered in the cornfield to kill the birds that eat young corn at this time of year. This fellow began showing symptoms, too, but hung his head and refused treatment. He disappeared into the woods, knowing he'd be blamed and probably severely punished for stealing. We often wonder if he survived.

Religious Practices

Nightly Christian Church Services

In the early fifties, Howard and Joan Law, Wycliffe Translators, were the first team to begin the long process of language analysis and Scripture translation in Nahuatl. Unfortunately, the Laws could not continue and had to return to the States in 1960 for medical reasons. Consequently, Scripture translation came to a halt.

A Spanish-speaking pastor from a Mexican Pentecostal denomination in the market town held services in Spanish but most of the Aztec people were monolingual and didn't understand Spanish. There were no written Scriptures in their Nahuatl language. Those who believed the Gospel started meeting in homes. The first Aztec Christians suffered persecution as a result of their testimonies. We never encountered any strong opposition to the Gospel during the years we lived there.

When we arrived, two Protestant groups were meet-

God's Talk

A typical church congregation in Mecayapan.

ing nightly--rain or shine. One group of twenty met in a thatched roof hut in the middle of the village, near our house. The other group met in a simple, rustic building on the other side of town with thirty or forty people in attendance. We did not attend services every night, but when we attended we alternated between the two groups. Our purpose was not to align ourselves with one particular group. Instead, we were there to ensure that everyone had access to the written Word on a non-sectarian basis.

For lighting, one or two kerosene lamps softly illuminated the earnest brown faces as they worshipped. The flickering flames of the lamps gave the whole room an ethereal radiance. There were rough hand-hewn back-less benches to sit on. It was hard to sit on a bench that long when the services often lasted three hours.

Religious Practices

Two young men strummed guitars, two or three fellows vigorously shook maracas, gourds and hand-made tambourines. The congregations loved to sing the Spanish hymns over and over. As they clapped fervently and sang with strident voices, the tempo and volume increased with each additional repetition until they were almost breathless. The many repetitions served a good purpose for them because, as pre-literate people, they learned the songs by repetition. Men and boys sat on one side of the building and women and girls on the other side. Each woman wore a head scarf or bandana as a head covering; her long, shiny black hair was braided neatly. Everybody rhythmically prayed out loud in Spanish at the same time, and they all stopped at the same time.

At one service our six-year-old neighbor boy, Victor, stood on the platform facing the audience wearing nothing but a wrinkled, blue-checked shirt. He joyfully hopped back and forth, first on one leg and then the other, keeping time with the lively music, oblivious to anyone else. The older boys competed against older girls as they recited Bible memory verses in Spanish.

As we talked with people after the services, it was obvious that they had minimal understanding of the Spanish they were hearing and speaking. We prayed for the time to come when they could sing, pray, preach and have the whole New Testament to read in Nahuatl, their heart-language.

(Ed. note: Our prayers were answered. At the time of this writing, at least twelve more congregations have formed over the entire Isthmus Aztec language area, and the Nahuatl Scriptures are widely used in the services.)

God's Talk

Carl describes our relationship to the churches:

Our aim was to be a witness in the community without formal affiliation with any group. Our relationships were good with all the leaders and we wanted to keep it that way. They were the ones who would make the most use of the translated Scriptures. I had hoped to have a regular time for Bible study with each of the church leaders, preferably all together, but it was hard to fit in with their daily field work and nightly meetings.

The group near our house soon built a new chapel with mud walls, tin roof, cement floor and a real door. They were very proud of it, and rightly so. They named it Ebenezer. It stood as a symbol of the cooperation they were beginning to develop. Most of the work was done on Sundays when they weren't out in their fields. I offered to make the sign and build a pulpit for them.

When Pastor Juan and his family transferred to a church near Lake Catamaco, Lucas took over the leadership of the Ebenezer Chapel. He asked me if I had any words of wisdom for him in his ministry so I shared some of my own experience with him. I encouraged him to use Nahuatl in the worship services as much as possible.

Many times we wondered: how much Spanish do they really understand? Is it just "vain repetition" to them? How would they talk about the Lord in Nahuatl if they could? There was a common belief that Spanish was a "spiritual" and "prestige" language. Some even thought God spoke only in Spanish and it would be sacrilegious and irreverent to use their own language because it had been so often labeled as gibberish by outsiders. Where did the Lord want us to fit in? How will Nahuatl Scripture be the greatest asset? In personal Bible study? Group worship? Bible classes? Lord, make us wise as serpents and

Religious Practices

harmless as doves, that we may gain their confidence and know the heart longings of the people.

Christmas Day 1967 seven people were baptized in the nearby mountain stream by one of the local preacher-boys. We distributed copies of the newly translated and printed Christmas story booklets to each group of believers, which by now had grown to four congregations. We detected a growing interest and pride in seeing their language in print for the first time. As God's Word in their language gained steady acceptance, we could see evidence of Him at work in their lives. They witnessed to others with new vigor. How much we take for granted by having many versions of the Bible in our own heart-language when people groups all over the world, like the Aztecs, don't even have **one** *version!*

Chencho, one of the very first believers, became a dedicated missionary to his own people. He carried the record player, Gospel records, songs and printed materials in Nahuatl along with him for weekend meetings in nearby towns. On his return, he reported conversions and a keen interest in **Itajtol Dios** *(God's Talk). This was music to our ears! More believers eagerly spread the Word and shared their faith in the Lord by taking the portable transistor record-players to capacity crowds at the thatched-roof meeting houses where many more heard the Gospel for the first time in their own language.*

Traditional Religious Practices

Many of the Aztecs continued to be steeped in their native beliefs, often based on fear. From our house we could see the huge, galvanized metal building across the plaza thet served as the local church. It had a dirt floor and a few rustic, home-made benches. One or two religious statues were

God's Talk

in it, and some older banners that hung near the lectern. These suggested it was a place of worship. The building was neglected since no resident priest was there to care for the people. On special saints' days someone was designated to beat the drums at intervals all night long--thrum, thrum, thrum--calling out various masses.

During Easter week, a group of the faithful would carry one of the church's religious images in a procession around the town. Drinking was a part of the occasion as it was for all village celebrations. On Easter morning they had another procession but the men carrying the flags were often very drink. One year Easter Sunday came and went without a flicker of activity in the nearby church. It was just like any other Sunday. It did not seem as though the people recognized the importance of the resurrection.

One summer, an itinerant Catholic priest and five student interns surprised the people by conducting a catechism class in Spanish three times a week to a small group of the children. They were friendly and visited with us several times. As far as we could tell, they did not generate any hostility toward us nor present any opposition. One was an American student from a Catholic seminary in Pennsylvania in the village for two weeks of practical experience. What seemed to take these men off their guard was that we were not there to preach, conduct church services or perform other ministerial functions. They expected to find us peddling our own particular brand of religion in a formal church setting. We assured them we were there to live among the people as friends and neighbors, learn the language, and translate the Bible and other literature.

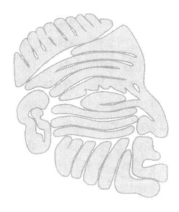

Beliefs and Customs of the People

As we adjusted to a new language and way of life, we inadvertently made many ignorant mistakes. We tried to tread softly and gently, learn as we went along, and be ready to laugh at ourselves when we butchered the language. Everyone was friendly, generous and helpful in so many ways. They accepted and loved us in spite of our bumbling and fumbling ways in a strange culture. Thankfully, our efforts paid off.

Being inquisitive about the culture was a very important part of understanding the people. Everything we could learn would be helpful later on as we got into translating the Bible. There was never a dull moment around this place. Involvement in people's daily lives always brought rewarding surprises. We recorded much of what we learned about the people's customs and beliefs. It was a stretch for us to thoroughly research a subject, asking questions without coming across as intrusive or arousing their suspicions about our motives. There were those who still believed we were there to steal their language and sell it back in the United States.

God's Talk

Several times a day women and children passed our house on the path to or from the river below. Babies were either balanced firmly on their hips or were carried in a *rebozo* (shawl) tied like a sling from their shoulders. On their heads they placed a rolled-up cloth in the shape of a doughnut. This provided a base for them to gracefully balance heavy loads of laundry in a metal basin, or a basket of cooked whole corn kernels (hominy, to us) to be rinsed in the river water and later ground into the day's tortillas, or an *olla* (clay water jar) or metal bucket full of water. It always amazed me how they did this without ever spilling any of the water! I often saw a woman carefully balance a big stalk of green bananas or load of firewood on her head. Only the women carried things this way. To learn this delicate balancing act a little girl as young as two years old practiced walking with an empty tin can on her head.

Young women and girls wore loose-fitting, home-made dresses. They walked barefooted everywhere. Older women retained the native costume of a blue-gray denim-like wrap-around skirt from the waist to the ankles, with nothing from the waist up, in other words, topless. On special occasions, like fiestas, they might add a blouse beautifully and intricately embroidered with large multi-colored flower designs.

Men and boys wore a native-style sandal called *huarache*. One day when Carl tore his trousers that I had already patched four times, he remarked to one of the fellows that now this pair was "done for." The fellow said, "When you're finished with them, I'll buy them." They wore patched clothes until they were more holes than clothes!

On chilly nights the temperature would dip to 55 degrees. We were almost painfully conscious of our warm comfortable beds, knowing that most of our friends around us were

Beliefs and Customs of the People

sleeping on dirt floors or a bamboo platform with only a thin woven straw mat *(petate)* beneath them. They had few possessions and were fortunate if they had a blanket or shawl to wrap around them to keep them warm. Small wonder many needed treatment for fevers and coughs.

In 1970 a fellow from one of the larger towns installed a gasoline-powered corn grinder and started up his own corn-grinding business in Mecayapan. Women stood in line with their baskets of whole cooked corn kernels, ready to have it ground into tortilla dough. This was quite a technological innovation for the women. Corn had been ground by hand on their *metates* (grinding stones) for centuries. I overheard one man say, "If someone would start up a tortilla-making machine, too, then a man won't have to look for a wife anymore; he could just go buy his tortillas."

One general belief was if a person was too thin he/she might either be sick, be something other than human or have a demon. The more affluent families were chubbier than those who had to forage for a living. For them the ideal was to be short and plump; being chubby meant you were more affluent as well as healthier. When Joan Law came to visit us, the women who had known her when she and her family lived there exclaimed how much heavier she was than before. "Now you are really pretty--so nice and fat!" they said. That's how they accepted me, too--so nice and fat.

Carl mentions other beliefs:

> *Some people have the custom of eating dirt from a certain place outside of town. I've heard that people who eat dirt lack certain chemicals or minerals in their diet. Intestinal parasites cause a craving for dirt and may explain the custom. We never could find out why they chose this certain kind of dirt. Some boys*

God's Talk

showed me a special place along the trail where dirt had been carved out of the bank. In the excavation there was a small flat rock used for digging. "Here they get dirt to eat. They take the dirt home, dry it, grind it fine and eat it. People crave it and say it tastes good to them," they said.

One fellow told me how they train a mule to not run away when you let go of the rope. The secret, he said, was to rub the animal's nose with a woman's urine. Some beliefs are truly unexplainable and imponderable!

As we locked up the house before we left to go to workshop for several weeks, Carl casually commented to some of the men standing around that our house had never been broken into while we were gone. One fellow spoke up and said, "People are afraid of the bones Señor Guillermo (Mr. Howard Law) has stored in a box there!" (When the Laws first came to the area in 1945 the people were very suspicious and circulated rumors that "the white man eats people"!) Carl reassured him there were no bones stored there. Ironically, it turned out, while we were away that time, the house <u>was</u> broken into and our saddle was stolen. We never retrieved it. We should have allowed that superstition to stay alive!

Our Aztec friends ate everything we gave them. We discovered they believe that if you look at food and don't eat it, it can make you sick.

One day several of my friends and I were sitting around our cozy fireplace. I shared that when I was a little girl and told my mother a lie, she washed my mouth out with soap. This struck them as terribly funny. They could hardly stop laughing. They proceeded to tell me if a child lied, the custom was to smear his/her mouth with horse manure or stuff a hot boiled egg, shell and all in his/her mouth,. This latter method is also used to punish a dog caught stealing eggs from someone's house.

They have a strong, imbedded belief that if they are taking medicine, it is bad for them to eat pork. During certain holidays the women and girls made the tastiest corn tamales by putting a small amount of spicy, shredded, cooked pork inside each one. So only the very sick people came to buy medicine during fiestas. Everyone preferred tamales over medicine unless they were too sick to eat at all. Friends usually brought delicious tamales to us or else invited us to their homes to share tamales and coffee with them.

Married Aztec women never used their given names and it was an insult to ask what their names were. An adult woman was addressed as someone's mother, usually the oldest child. For example, the women didn't call me Maria Elena (Marilyn); they called me *iye Carolina*, (mother of Carrie). The same went for the father, *itaj Carolina* (father of Carrie). At first I tried to keep medical records on my patients who came regularly for treatment. It turned out to be an exercise in futility since the kinship system was very complicated.

Associations and Beliefs Strange to Us

- When a baby died of diarrhea the mother thought it was caused by a quarrel two girls had at the water-hole.
- People associated an infected wound with being embarrassed or emotionally upset.
- A group of men and boys took turns looking at the moon with the binoculars. They believe that the moon is made of silver and is pasted up against the sky. They asked Carl, "What keeps it from falling out of the sky?"

God's Talk

- If you admire a baby or small child and say how pretty he/she is but fail to caress or hold him/her in your arms, they believe you cast an "evil eye" on the child. In two or three days the mother will report that the child has developed a headache and its eyes have filled with pus.

I further explored the meaning of the phrases "to give the evil eye" or to "cast a spell" on someone. Originally, I had understood that I should <u>not</u> caress or hold their children for fear of frightening them more than they already were, since children were told to be afraid of the "white lady." When I found out what it <u>really</u> meant, my knees felt weak. Many times I had told a mother how pretty and fat her baby was but refrained from touching it or holding it. I asked Sylvia, my language helper, if anyone had ever complained that I gave their baby an "evil eye." She said one mother told her I had. She then soaked a special leaf in water overnight and the next morning bathed the baby's head with that water so that "the pain in its head would go away."

Mothers do not put diapers on their infants. Instead, the baby is carried naked with only a rag held loosely around its bottom. The wet rag is replaced with a dry one when necessary. I decided they have the right idea--I never saw a case of diaper rash. Visiting one of my sick patients at home, I saw a plump, six month-old baby laughing so I asked if I could hold him. The older sister reluctantly gave him to me then anxiously hovered over me while I bounced him on my knees. Was she scared that I would do something to him? Later, Sylvia explained: "She was afraid he would wet on you; then you would be just like us!"

Beliefs and Customs of the People

One day a young mother came to ask for a piece of bread. I asked her if that's what she was hungry for. She said, "No, I've been nauseated lately, and someone told me that if I tie an egg and a bread roll around my middle it might keep me from feeling nauseated." Since I knew her quite well, I said, jokingly, "It might help you more if you would **eat** the bread." By her facial expression, I don't think she was convinced or caught my humor. Probably it was another one of their centuries-old beliefs. Anyway, I gave her one of my fresh-baked rolls. She left happy.

Ever wonder how the indigenous people "potty-train" a child? From my kitchen window I watched my neighbor teach little two-year-old Anna to squat **outside** the house instead of **inside**. Later she would teach her to go to "the bushes" a short distance away from the house.

One of the first items we brought for our house was a big fifty-gallon barrel for catching roof water when it rained. After a particularly vicious rain and thunderstorm, Carl commented to our neighbor across the back yard fence about damage done by the lightning to our tall radio antenna the night before. Our neighbor, not yet a believer, said, with ominous overtones, "Maybe the thunder-maker hates your new rain barrel." Carl was able to tell him that when we believe God takes care of us, we need not be afraid. This was a classic example of their belief in cause and effect. They associated anything new or different that happens to us with something we might have done. Carl's testimony was reinforced the next day when he put up another antenna! People were awe-struck. If the foreigners are so powerful that they defy the god-powers that control the elements, who knows what they will do next?

God's Talk

Carl hears what people think of men on the moon:

People heard about the 1969 moon flight of Apollo Eleven on their radios and were quite puzzled about it all. One woman was afraid that they would break up the sky and make it fall on us. The night after the man walked on the moon we had a severe storm, heavy rain and lots of thunder and lightning. They reasoned, it was a direct result of men disturbing things on the moon by walking around up there.

The next night about 10:30 I felt a mild earth tremor that made the back door rattle. It happened just as I was falling asleep. I thought maybe it was the wind shaking the door or just my heartbeat shaking the bed. People in grass houses felt it too. They just knew it had something to do with walking around on the moon.

Interesting Cultural Items

- People color chicken's wings to identify who they belong to.
- They fill their mouth with water and spurt it out over their hands to wash them.
- The people walk six miles round trip to save 50 centavos on a kilo of salt, or five centavos on a bottle of kerosene.
- Death is the first thing they think about when we go away. They know there's a good chance they won't be here when we come back.
- Women nurse each other's babies.

Beliefs and Customs of the People

Interesting Associations

- She ate lemons and then her period stopped.
- He ate noodles and then his wound oozed more.
- She got a vitamin injection and asked if she should stay away from fire. (This related to the hot/cold sickness belief)
- Carrie was playing at the river with a wet skirt on when the lady said, "Oh, now her stomach will hurt!"

Photographs for the People

Our Polaroid camera became very popular and people were pleased to have a photo ready in a minute. Women, young girls and children often came for pictures dressed in their most colorful clothing and looking really beautiful. They asked if it cost more to take a picture of two people than just one person. They also wanted their whole body in the picture so their spirit wouldn't be divided. The town president asked if I would take a picture of him giving the school children the government-issued powdered milk and flour so he could prove that he actually gave it to them and didn't sell it. They liked to have their pictures taken, but when they had to scrape up the six pesos, it was another matter.

One evening we gave one of the neighbors a nice big ripe tomato from our garden. The next day the mother came with her little four-year-old girl all decked out in a pretty dress and ribbons in her hair, asking me to take her picture. And what did she want the little girl to hold in the picture? The red-ripe tomato we had given her. That made Carl puff up with pardonable pride!

Local Medicine Men

The first time I witnessed a person being treated by the local *curandero* (medicine man/healer), I felt the atmosphere in the shadowy hut was palpable with dark power. He went through an elaborate ritual of burning incense. Then he passed a freshly killed chicken several times over the flickering fire on the floor in the middle of the hut. Several times he waved the scorched chicken over the sick person while chanting something I couldn't understand. He took a handful of ashes from the fire and placed them on her forehead along with more chanting. The next day she died. Her son came to buy nails awhile later. That usually meant only one thing around here--they were building a box for her burial.

Sometimes people would seek help for their illnesses from the local healer first. If their symptoms got worse after that, they might come to me to see if my medicine would help them. Often by that time they had become sicker so what I could do for them medically was inadequate or useless.

Animals

Animals had free run of the entire village, going in and out of people's huts. Skinny, timid-looking dogs would slink warily around corners; fat, mother pigs with 8-10 piglets squealed and grunted as they foraged for food; turkeys and chickens gobbled and clucked as they pecked around for tidbits of corn dough dropped from the *metate* (grinding stone) where the *masa* (corn dough) was being patted into tortillas.

We were surprised at how roughly this normally peaceful people could treat animals. Dogs especially, so skinny you could count their ribs, were often dealt cruel blows. They

Beliefs and Customs of the People

beat a dog mercilessly or pick it up by the tail and throw it against the side of a wall as punishment for some minor misdemeanor.

They took very good care of their horses, mules and burros, though. One stormy night while the rain pounded for hours, our nearest neighbors brought their horse into their grass-roofed hut. That big horse took up almost a quarter of the tiny hut's floor space. Pablo had a supply of grass for him to munch on calmly while the family slept.

The Hut-moving Process

Several thatch-roofed huts were in the path of the four new streets that were being graded down through the middle of the town. All of the huts had to be moved or they would have ended up being in the middle of the new street.

The process of moving a thatched-roof hut from one location to another was quite an unusual sight. The owner first planted four new corner posts at the next location. Forty or fifty local men gathered underneath the roof of the hut and at a given signal they all positioned one of their shoulders under the cross-beams. Amid much shouting and swearing, when all were ready to go forward, the roof swayed and creaked as they carried it slowly along the path to the new corner posts. The only visible movement under the thatch roof was all those legs shuffling along!

One roof they tried to move was badly eaten by termites. No sooner had the men lifted it off its moorings than it began to slide to one side. The men on the lower side quickly propped it up long enough to allow all of them to get out from under it before it went CRASH! It laid there in a dejected-looking

God's Talk

heap of sticks and grass. The women all ran out of their huts weeping and wailing that their men were being killed. Such a hullabaloo! Luckily only one man suffered an injury--a nasty gash in his finger that required stitches at my porch-clinic.

Fiestas

November 1-2 is the traditional two-day annual holiday of All-Saints' Day--a major celebration all over Mexico. There is always a big fiesta with a colorful parade and good food to eat. Carl was up at 2:30 a.m. for the hog-butchering ceremony over at Pablo's house. I canned three pints of pork and we enjoyed some extra for dinner. Women make dozens of corn tamales with a bit of pork inside. To make tamales they spread a glob of cooked corn dough on a banana leaf and spread a spoonful of cooked shredded pork seasoned with *chile* and *acoyo* leaf on the corn dough. Then the banana leaf is wrapped around the dough. It resembles a big dumpling.

The six dozen or more tamales are stacked in a special pattern on top of each other in a large clay pot or in a five gallon can, with a couple inches of water in the bottom. They are then covered and steamed all night over a carefully tended open fire. Next morning, the custom is to take some of them to the cemetery for the spirits of their dead ancestors to eat. In the evening, as we took a walk around town. The family fires were being tended, people were laughing, talking, and singing, and preparations were being made for the dozens of tamales each family would consume during the festivities.

A religious festival took place each year in June when St. James, the patron saint of Mecayapan, was honored with two big fiesta days. People from many other Aztec towns came for the festivities. Several priests came who were in charge of the ceremonies. One of them was a young American studying in Mexico. We invited him to eat hamburgers with us one day. He said he hadn't eaten such a good hamburger for a long time!

Out of curiosity, I walked across the plaza later to see what was going on at the big Catholic church at fiesta time. The number of inebriated men staggering around didn't surprise me since liquor flowed freely at these events. One obnoxious man, who obviously had too much to drink, insisted on sitting down at a table where the beer and "firewater" were being served. The lady in charge of that stand went after him with a big stick. Then he picked up another stick and went after <u>her</u>. An onlooker deftly grabbed the man's stick from behind. The lady then coolly filled a pan with water and doused the drunk man. But he wasn't easily discouraged and kept coming back. She managed to throw six or seven pans of water at him before he finally decided to walk away. This melee attracted quite a crowd and everybody cheered loudly every time she scored a direct hit!

Weddings

Marriages were officially arranged between the girl's father and the boy's father without the girl or boy ever having met or spoken to each other. The marriageable age was any time after age thirteen. After we had lived there eight and a half years it felt like twice that long when we were invited to the weddings of young people who were only six or seven years old when we came.

January was the month for weddings. That was when people had the most money from selling their coffee beans, black

God's Talk

beans, corn and maybe a cow. The proceeds from these were used to pay the bride-price. These festivities were very interesting occasions with lots of cultural nuances.

We were invited to attend one of these occasions on a balmy evening. A bright, full moon heightened the excitement of the festive atmosphere. The silvery moonlight shone down through the trees giving the milling crowd a romantic aura.

Four women were grinding tortilla dough on four *metates* (grinding stones) next to four small fires under the trees. Four *comales* (clay griddles) were each delicately balanced on three stones above the fires. The tortilla dough was patted out into flat 10 inch tortillas, and then at just the right intervals, each woman expertly pushed sticks of firewood in to the center of her fire to maintain the perfect temperature for the tortillas to cook. With an experienced slap, the tortillas were plonked down, one at a time, on to the hot clay griddles and cooked three to five minutes, turned at just the right time to insure being cooked through. These four women could make enough soft, tender tortillas for 80 people.

We joined several guests seated under a canvas awning on rustic wooden benches around an equally rustic wooden table. Two large clay pots, balanced on three stones over glowing coals, were full of simmering *coyame'mol* (pork gravy). The delicious dish was served to each guest in enamel bowls to be eaten with warm tortillas (no spoons), and they were given cups of weak coffee to drink. There is a skill to eating gravy without spoons, though. It was tricky at first till we got the hang of it. Tear a tortilla in fourths, double one quarter to create a spoon-like utensil, then dip into the gravy, and ...voilá! Eat it--"spoon" and all.

Where was the bride all this time? Sitting in a corner of her future mother in law's house where, according to their tradition, she was expected to stay out of sight. She put on her saddest, most embarrassed, pouting expression while the groom was having a merry time dancing with his guests to the music of a mariachi band on the crude homemade platform. A few guests stood around enjoying the social atmosphere while others danced. The dancing would go on all night. There was plenty of tepid beer and free-flowing *aguardiente* (firewater), the powerful, home-brewed liquor of fermented sugar cane juice.

On another occasion, our neighbor lady, who did our laundry, asked me to help Rosa get dressed for her marriage to her son Calistro. I followed her to Rosa's house. First of all, her mother offered us soft drinks. Rosa was petulant and adamantly refused to cooperate. I was a novice at this so I wondered what I was supposed to do next. Her mother said I should just put on her dress and veil, shoes and socks whether she wanted to or not. In the process of doing that, Rosa went as limp as a rag doll--I even had to lift her arms to put the dress on!

After she was properly dressed, I was to walk with her and the rest of the family in a procession to the town secretary's office. In Mexico, time is relative--we waited for at least an hour before the town President and Secretary arrived to perform the legal ceremony. It was obvious they had been

God's Talk

drinking. After the ceremony, the bride and groom each went to their respective homes until the next day.

Preparations for a grand two-day celebration continued. Guests brought hand-woven baskets full of gifts for the young couple and placed them on the ground inside the circle. There must have been twenty baskets, each filled with identical items: ears of dried corn, soap powder, cloth yardage and salt. Our gift was a brightly colored plaid wool blanket to keep them warm at night.

Men carried in crates of soft drinks and beer. Chairs gathered from neighbors were placed in a circle next to Calistro's hut. His mother carried a basket with six roasted chickens in it and placed it on the patio of the bride's hut. Stacks of firewood were carried in to keep cooking fires going. Corn tortillas were patted out, and a large quantity of *bebida* was made in clay pots. This was a sweetened, roasted corn drink that tasted like Postum. As chicken and rice were served with tortillas, women sat on one side and men on the other. Pop and beer were passed around to each guest.

It was considered discourteous to the host to refuse beverages that the host offered. Most wedding guests could devour three or more bottles of pop in quick succession. It must be a learned skill because I could never get more than two down. I discovered that each woman had a jar tucked under her shawl. If she was already full of pop, she poured the contents of the next bottles into that jar to enjoy later. I took mental note for the next time I went to a wedding.

At this point the spokesman or "marriage ambassador" greeted the group, presented the bride-price money to her father followed by the traditional ceremony, *mohuexitiaj*, (binding the two families into their in-law relationship).

Beliefs and Customs of the People

Then came more pop/beer-guzzling as the groom went around the circle to receive advice and a handshake blessing. All throughout these ceremonial matters, the bride was isolated in her parents' hut.

About 1:00 p.m. it was time for me to accompany the bride to this gathering. She was even more reluctant than the day before. Two of us got on each side, took her by her arms and practically dragged her to the groom's house. I often wondered about this custom for the bride to be resistant and non-compliant. Was a 13-year-old bride just following tradition or did she truly feel embarrassed and hesitant to begin a new relationship? It was late evening when the groom finally received his bride and everyone went home.

At Benito's wedding Carl and I were given the honor of going with the groom's parents to get the bride, Anatolia, at her house on the other side of town. We arrived at the appointed hour and were told she and her mother had gone to the river. They would be back "anytime." For one and a half hours we waited while being offered bottle after bottle of warm Pepsi. Her father finally went to see what was taking them so long. When he brought her back to the house she was crying her eyes out. Being only 14, I couldn't blame her for not wanting to leave home and live with someone she's never spoken to before.

When I showed her the new outfit of clothes furnished by the groom's parents, she just stared at them--wouldn't even lift a finger to help put them on. As I had done for other brides, I dressed her right down to putting on the new shoes, socks, earrings and necklace, braiding her hair and pinning on the pretty lace veil. In spite of her passive resistance, constant sniffling and wiping tears, she finally agreed to walk with us the half mile to the town office for the civil ceremony.

With her head bowed, (from embarrassment?), it took fifteen minutes of persuasion before Anatolia mumbled a nearly inaudible affirmative, "Mmmm," after the town secretary asked her, "Are you willing to take this man for your husband?" There, in the presence of four witnesses and several family members, the bride and groom were legally married. All the official documents were then signed by the groom, and finger-printed by the bride. She never learned to write. The wedding procession traipsed back to the bride's hut where we were treated to more *al tiempo* (room temperature) soft drinks.

The next day, enthusiastic feasting and merrymaking went on at the groom's hut before his parents brought the bride and groom to live with them for at least a year. Traditionally, she becomes like their daughter and his mother teaches her how to please her young husband by making his tortillas the way he likes them. A year later the young couple builds a hut of their own near his parents.

Childbirth

Three native midwives seemed quite capable so it didn't seem necessary for me to upset their way of doing things. They often asked me for an injection that would give the mother "strength" when she was exhausted from a lengthy labor. I would give a double dose of vitamins and iron, mixed with Vitamin K which I knew they needed anyway. The psychological effect was such that usually within a half hour the baby was born!

Beliefs and Customs of the People

Childbirth Customs

Four months after we arrived one of the midwives came to ask me to give Pastor John's wife, Maria, an injection for "strength." She was exhausted having been in labor for several hours. She said, "The baby doesn't want to come out."

When a woman is in labor she kneels on a straw mat spread on the dirt floor. A stout rope secured from a rafter is in front of her. With every contraction she pulls down on the rope. At the same time, someone, often the husband, squats behind her and, during each contraction, tightens a cloth tied around her waist. This acts something like a tourniquet, helping to push the baby downward. The local midwife is by her side giving instructions.

Maria was in the above position when I arrived on the scene. I gave her a low dose of sedative to help her relax and an injection of vitamins, liver extract and vitamin K and suggested she lie down as she was very tired. Four or five women stood around, each offering to help. One tended a little fire close to the patient. Another rubbed her tummy, arms and legs with the oil squeezed from the seeds of the *zapote* fruit. Pastor John paced in and out of the hut, obviously feeling helpless in the presence of all the women.

They ushered me in where they were circled around her praying. It was getting dark and the hut was dimly lit by a kerosene lamp. She was very weak by this time. I told them I couldn't guarantee the injection would increase her

God's Talk

"strength." But then I often underestimated the psychological effect medicines have on people.

I was so interested in all the proceedings but didn't want to get in the way, so I stood in a shadowy corner of the hut. After she rested awhile on the cot, she got into position again, on her knees, holding on to the rope tightly while the native midwife continued with the belt-tightening and prepared to receive the baby as it emerged. In a matter of about 10 minutes she had several strong contractions that she was able to work along with this time. Out came the baby with the cord wrapped twice around the neck. Skillfully and swiftly the midwife untangled the cord and delivered the placenta almost at the same time.

Since her first two babies had been stillborn we didn't know what her chances were this time. The suspense hung heavy over the little group around her. All of us were praying the baby would be born alive. I prayed fervently under my breath that the midwife would know what she was doing. I wasn't sure if I was crying or if the acrid smoke from the little fire was causing tears to cascade down my cheeks. Probably a little of both. Ah, the baby boy was alive and breathing! I guessed he weighed about four and a half pounds. Such a cacophony of speech I couldn't understand!

The midwife laid the baby on one pile of clean clothes and the afterbirth on another. I wondered when she would cut the cord. The baby was ignored for a few minutes while they bathed Maria, put clean clothes on her, tied a cloth around her head and eased her back on to the cot. Pastor John came in to embrace his wife and give support while they dressed her. After she was cleaned and dressed they turned their attention to the baby lying there looking around and making little sucking sounds, still attached to the placenta!

Beliefs and Customs of the People

I was absolutely flabbergasted and amazed to discover nothing was available to cut the cord. No one seemed to be in a big hurry, either. Finally, the midwife sent one of the ladies to look for a scissors, sewing thread and cotton fabric. All these were produced from someone else's hut in a matter of two or three minutes. She deftly tied the cord, but had difficulty cutting it as the scissors were very dull. She ordered someone to heat a machete blade until red-hot over the small fire still burning. This took another couple minutes. She used it to cut the cord and sterilize the end of it. I breathed a prayer of thanks that she knew enough to prevent infection from unsterile scissors. She then put cotton over the cord, laid a clean cloth over it, put a tummy binder on the baby and laid him beside his mother. So far so good. What would they put on to keep him warm? Someone rummaged through a heap of clothes in the corner and found a little cap and flannel jacket to put on the baby.

About this time they discovered I was still huddled in my corner watching this scenario. They all began exclaiming what a good injection it was that I gave her. "It gave her that extra strength she needed right at the last five minutes!" We all agreed that prayer was mighty important, too, and that God was good to bring the baby out alive. They asked me about how we give birth to children in our country. I said "It's a long story. Maybe I'll tell you sometime."

All this hustle and bustle of activity was carried out with a great deal of animated conversation and high-pitched laughter as they cracked jokes and told funny stories. When I left, preparations were being made to cook a big rooster and have a "feed." Everyone was happy. People poked their heads inside the hut to get a peek at the new baby. Soon after I came home, Pastor John stopped by and I asked if he had eaten supper yet. He said, "No." I offered him a plate of beans, tortillas and chocolate cake left from our supper. He devoured it with gusto that matched his previous excitement and frantic pacing.

I am still amazed at the contrast between the high risk of contamination in the village compared to the super-sterile conditions we strive for in the state-side hospitals. It is so far removed from the cool, calm efficiency of a hospital delivery room. But this is the method used by four fifths of the world population that live in primitive conditions.

Observations at Other Birthing Occasions

A sister stood beside the mother and poked a finger down her throat to make her retch. When that didn't work she took a wad of her hair and crammed it down her sister's throat to make her gag. Was this done to hasten the birth? I was repulsed the first time I saw what seemed to me to be a very crude method, but they took it as a matter of stated policy.

The newborn is placed on a pile of rags and left uncovered 15-20 minutes until the placenta is delivered and the cord is cut. Such a scurrying around for rags to wrap the baby in. The midwife started to wrap it in an old pair of trousers when someone else said, "That's too rough, here's something softer." So a worn-out dress was used instead.

No one seems to make any preparation for the event. (My theory is that infant mortality is so high they think the baby might not live very long.) Someone is sent to another house to borrow thread, a razor blade, cotton fabric, etc. Some one asks the father, who has been standing outside all this time, to find a bag to put the placenta in. It is later buried carefully in the ground beside the house.

Beliefs and Customs of the People

The midwife ties the umbilical cord, reaches behind her for an ear of dried corn, places the cord over the ear of corn and cuts through it with the not-too-sharp razor blade or machete that may or may not have been passed through the fire to sterilize it. The belief is that the ear of corn will insure fertility.

On one occasion when the little girls were told they could come in and see their baby sister. They tiptoed in holding each other's hands. Their aunt said to them, "Go over there and see the little worm! Over there it is, just a worm!" Before it is given a name, I guess that's how they think of it.

When Nemorio's wife was in labor, he offered Silvia and me a soft drink, but he offered beer to the four elderly ladies that helped the birth along. All but one accepted. She told him she was taking vitamin tonic so maybe she shouldn't drink beer. Then she turned to me and asked "Do you think it is bad to drink beer when I am taking tonic?" I said (tongue in cheek), "Yes, it's bad," not wanting to address this controversial issue just then. The three ladies drank more beer before eating the beans and tortillas offered them. By the time we left they were quite happy!

Valentino's wife was about to give birth when he came to ask for a vitamin injection for the "extra strength" she needed. He said he was on his way to Soteapan to buy some clothes and would stop on his way back. I assumed the clothes would be for the baby. When he returned, I went with him to give my special combination of vitamins. Later that day I hiked up to their hut to check on his wife. She was sitting cross-legged beside a small fire on a straw mat spread over the dirt floor. A healthy baby boy, wrapped in a strip of fabric, was lying on a pile of clean rags. I was astonished to see Valentino and his wife were the ones who had the new clothes on. This culture was full of surprises!

The conversation frequently shifted to them asking me if this is the way I had to suffer when I delivered my daughter, Carrie. Then it progressed on to the fact that I have only one child and the possible reasons for it. Did I have an operation? Did I take pills? Oh, of course. I must take pills if I didn't have an operation. This time, though, one lady said, "God must love you," meaning she wished they wouldn't have so many children.

Death and Funerals

Acceptance of death as part of the life cycle was a cultural norm among the people. It was a stark contrast to modern medical measures that tend to prolong the dying process. Here they were inclined to let nature take its course--no heroics beyond seeking a minimum of medicine. This was partly due to the language barrier, economic costs of services and long distances to modern medical facilities.

We had a unique business--selling medicine to help people get well and, on a few occasions, selling lumber to make their simple wooden coffins when they die. Some people had a vague idea of Christ's death and resurrection. However, they lived in such darkness of true spiritual understanding. Gradually we understood the customs and beliefs they have about evil spirits, the devil, visions and God.

Everyone was sad as a little two-year-old boy was prepared for burial on Easter morning. Carl was asked to read Scripture and speak of the meaning of Easter and the resurrection. We arrived at the house just as they were nailing the wooden box shut. The mother carefully put a plate, a cup, a few tortillas wrapped in a cloth and some money beside the body. The belief was that the person will need these in the next life. A small procession of relatives followed as the tiny box was carried on two men's shoulders out to the cemetery.

Chimino's wife, very pale and sick for several months, died one morning about 10:00 o'clock leaving three little children motherless. Such was life and death in this remote setting. She had believed God's Talk so the family was comforted that her suffering was over and her soul was with the Lord. The three of us attended the all-night wake with her body laid out on a cot. Carl helped the men nail the boards together to make the coffin. Some young fellows strummed guitars, sang hymns, read Scripture and listened to the Nahuatl hymns on the records. Women ground corn for tortillas to be served at midnight with the roasted corn drink (*bebida*). Others wept silently, teenage girls chattered and had giggling spells, smaller children fell asleep on the *petates* (straw mats) spread out on the dirt floor.

Carl writes of a sad outcome:

His nickname was Shorty and he was minus two front teeth. He lived on the other side of the creek and often came to visit us. One rainy morning at 7:00 a.m. he wanted an injection "for strength" for his wife who was in labor. Marilyn was ready to go with him, but he said, "Wait till I send my little girl over." He would be embarrassed to be seen walking with a woman.

More than an hour passed and no one came so we figured everything turned out all right. Later in the afternoon, much to our dismay, he came for boards to make a box--for his wife! I could hardly believe my ears. But the tears on his face told me that he wasn't joking. Next morning I happened to look out our front door and saw the silent procession carry her body to the cemetery. I discovered later that someone else in town had given her three injections (we don't know who or what). Then I found out that he **had** sent his child to call me, but she dawdled on the way and never arrived at our house. It may not have made a scintilla of difference in the outcome. We'll never know. The baby boy was given to a mother who still had breast milk. The two older children were cared for by relatives.

Christmas Holiday Customs

Very low key! Christmas trees, gift exchange or decorations in their homes were unheard of in this culture.

Our first Christmas, Pastor John, in traditional Mexican custom, encouraged the believers to decorate the thatch-roof chapel with a small tree, balloons, shiny tinfoil objects and Spanish moss draped all around. As the afternoon sun streamed through the split pole walls it really did look quite festive. On Christmas Eve they had church services featuring songs and Scripture--fifty or more people attended. They sang and worshipped until 5:00 a.m. followed by a big tamale feast.

Local Agriculture

In the backwater areas of Mexico most tribal people raised their crops much the same way their ancestors must have done hundreds of years ago. Crops were planted using the ancient custom of poking holes in the earth several inches apart with a pointed dibble stick. Then two or three seeds were dropped in the hole and were covered with soil. A few people who were a bit more prosperous cultivated their fields with a crudely built wooden plow pulled by one or

Beliefs and Customs of the People

Coffee beans (in the foreground) and black beans (rear) are spread on canvas or on the bare ground to dry thoroughly before bagging for sale.

---

two oxen. The hilly, rocky terrain did not lend itself to modern machinery so no one owned farm machinery like tractors. Their entire lives revolved around planting and harvesting seasons.

In the spring, they were busy harvesting coffee beans that were ripe for picking. Coffee is a major cash crop for them. They also planted bananas, pineapples, squash and a few other vegetables. Corn and black beans were the main staples. They would get two, maybe three, crops of corn a year. The people harvested their big cash crop of black beans in January by pulling up the dry bean stalks, roots and all. They piled the unshelled dry bean stalks on a large canvas tarp and flailed them with big sticks so that the beans broke out of their shells and rattled down to the tarp, probably

God's Talk

much like Bible times threshing grain. The shells and stalks were then discarded.

When the wind was just right, they put the beans and the chaff in a basket, held the basket about three feet off the tarp, then tipped it so the beans spilled out slowly on to the tarp, and they let the wind blow away the chaff. The winnowed beans landed in a neat pile and were bagged in burlap sacks, ready to take to market or sell at the store in Soteapan where they brought a good price.

Rumors: Hail vs. Smallpox

Soon after we returned from the 1967 workshop terrible rumors got started around town.

1. We brought smallpox back with us to the village,

2. Carrie was all covered with it,

3. She had been very sick,

4. We brought her back in a box.

In one section of town the older women were wailing in an uproar over it. They remembered the terrible cases of smallpox in the village before vaccinations. The town president told Carl that some drunken men came to his door that morning and said, "We might as well enjoy ourselves, we're all going to die of smallpox anyway." They threatened to

Beliefs and Customs of the People

chase us out of town and then burn our house with everything in it.

At first we were totally mystified how or why such a rumor got started. The threat to chase us out of the village and burn our house down was a malicious attack against us. Those who passed the rumor around were unbelievers resistant to the Gospel, so we wondered if it was a Satanic attack now that the Word of God was being brought to the people in a form they easily understood.

Immediately Silvia took Carrie personally around town to show them she was well and healthy with a vaccination scar to prove she'll never have smallpox. They walked over to the far edge of town and sure enough, women there were crying and wailing, but when they saw that Carrie was alive and had clear, smooth skin, they calmed down right away.

In Nahuatl the words for rain, hail and smallpox are very similar except the length is on different vowels. In the word "smallpox" the length is on the first syllable and in "hail" it is on the second syllable. Carl remembered that one evening he had jokingly told a crowd of men standing around that maybe we brought the rain. (It had rained day and night for over a week after we got back--14.2 inches in 12 days.)

After piecing all the fragments together, Carl concluded he had lengthened the wrong vowel when he talked about how it had rained and hailed where we were at the workshop. He must have said *"quiahua'"* (hail) and it came out sounding like *"quiahua*a**"** (smallpox). We were still far from being fluent in the language so it was easy to inadvertently lengthen or shorten the wrong syllable.

God's Talk

The smallpox scare died down in a couple of days, but we were painfully reminded how intricately languages are constructed and also how delicate our relationship to the people can be.

Our theory was that someone in the crowd heard it incorrectly and then fabricated the other parts of the gossip. Would that the gospel be spread around and believed that easily. Gossip could be good if the <u>right</u> things got started!

Rain, Rain, Rain

The yearly rainfall was estimated to be from 100-120 inches a year in this part of the tropics. During the rainy season, June-January, we battled thick, gooey mud everywhere. When the men went to cut roof-grass for someone's new house, they walked through torrential, tropical rain and came home soaked to the skin. Usually the rains were warm but when a cold "*norte*" (storm from the north) blew in with rain, rain and more rain the cold winds penetrated every pore of our bodies. It often rained five or six inches at night. A very noisy thunderstorm and torrential rain made a deafening noise on the tin roof of the house. It was so loud that Carrie came down from her bed in the loft to crawl in bed with us.

After being away six weeks at a workshop, we came home the day the trail was fairly dry. We could see the storm clouds brewing but the rain held off long enough for us to get most of our baggage hauled in by mules. While we were gone, we weren't exactly practicing our mountain climbing exercises so we huffed and puffed up and down the hills. Carl even made a second trip to Soteapan to get the remainder of our baggage, which meant he walked 10 miles, at least, that day between 11:00 a.m. and 6:00 p.m. He was ready to hit the sack at bedtime.

The worst electrical storm happened one night just before we retired. Great sheets of lightning struck our radio antenna pole, split it right down the middle and shattered it into slivers. We watched as a fire ball melted the antenna wire clear into the house with a terrifying, deafening sound as if the whole house would blow up. In four hours it rained four and a half inches. The radio was essential to communicate with our colleagues in Mexico City headquarters and Oaxaca, so the next day, much to the amazement and consternation of the neighbors, we erected another antenna pole. They said we were defying the thunder-god!

Trail Trips, River Crossings, Shopping Excursions

Carl describes the trail:

Preparation for travel in this tropical, mountainous part of the country was a lot more complicated than hopping in the car to go shopping or take a vacation. At the end of the paved road in Soteapan we park our car and take the foot trail that descends sharply to the first stream. We cross carefully by stepping on the smooth, slippery stones, balancing ourselves and maybe a heavy backpack too. With a load on one's back it's quite a trick because some places in the water are knee deep. A hike up the bank on the other side takes us over a ridge and down to the big Huasuntlan river 200 feet wide with clear, rushing water. Shoes off and pants rolled up, we cross over the stones cautiously and then rest awhile on the other side. This river can

Rain, Rain, Rain

isolate Mecayapan from Soteapan when it rises to powerful proportions after a heavy rain, making it uncrossable.

We scramble up this steep river bank and the trail levels off for a couple of miles through a wooded area, some scrub oak and tall grassland. Finally we descend to the shallow, 50 foot wide stream that borders Mecayapan. This one is easy to cross on stepping stones and then climb up the stream bank. As darkness descends, we plod on to our house using our trusty flashlight, which is standard equipment on any trip.

Carl writes of complications to the shopping trip:

Shopping day in Acayucan: Our monthly check from headquarters hadn't arrived yet and our food and medical supplies were running low. Another fellow and I decided to hike to Soteapan hoping the check would be in the mail. It had rained during the night, and the big river had risen so much that by the time we got there it was too deep and wide to wade across. As we stood on the river bank wondering what to do next, two fellows on horseback came by on their way to Soteapan. Their horses would be able to cross so they offered to pick up our mail for us and return soon. We decided to trudge back over the trail to Mecayapan. Those guys never did show up that day.

Next day, the river had receded enough that we could cross on foot. Three of the brethren and I decided to go to Acayucan even if our money didn't come. I had only 10 pesos in my pocket, which wouldn't go very far. But the men agreed to help buy gas if our check didn't arrive and carry any purchases back home for me if it did. At the post office I was very disappointed that the check was not waiting for me, but amazingly, before we arrived in Acayucan, I had the check in my hand.

God's Talk

Here's how it happened:

The Lind family had arranged to meet me in Soteapan and we agreed we would drive together to Acayucan but in separate vehicles. They were delayed, and because their <u>radio</u> battery had died, they couldn't send me a message. When I got to our car in Soteapan, I discovered the <u>car</u> battery was dead. When Linds finally arrived they pushed our car down the hill to get it started and we were both off on our shopping trip.

A few miles down the road, we stopped in Chinameca at the electric service so Linds could charge their radio battery. Just then the second-class bus pulled up at the gas station across the road and out popped the town secretary from Mecayapan, waving his arms at me and pointing at his briefcase. I walked over and noticed that his briefcase was loaded with mail. Shuffling through it he picked out a half-dozen letters for us but none that had the check in it. "I think that's all," he said. Again my heart sank with disappointment--our check was not there. Then I happened to spy another envelope in his case with our headquarters return address: Instituto Linguistico de Verano. That was it--our check! So now we could do our much-needed shopping. Had Linds not had to charge their radio battery, we never would have stopped at Chinameca and would have missed getting our check. Another example of God's perfect timing.

We arrived in Acayucan by 11:00 a.m. Most stores close at 1:00 o'clock for the customary two-hour siesta so there was no time to waste. I hurriedly made my purchases at the grocery store and lumber yard, including two bundles of corrugated galvanized roofing for our new porch. Two boys carried six boxes of groceries to our car and secured the sheet metal on to Lind's roof rack.

Rain, Rain, Rain

The pharmacy and fresh produce market stay open all afternoon so I bought medicines, medical supplies, and a few fresh vegetables. My lunch at the market consisted of a large steaming bowl of beef and vegetables, eight hot tortillas and a bottle of pop for only 40 cents U.S. That satisfied my hunger. Surprisingly, we all gathered at the car about the same time. Pablo suddenly decided he needed to buy a food grinder, so he took off for the store again, and Epifaneo remembered he wanted to buy some cookies. Soon everybody was ready to wend our way home.

The store keeper in Soteapan offered to keep the metal roofing for me until I came back the next day with a mule to carry it. We had no pack animals to carry the cargo this time so the boxes were distributed on the backs of us four men and secured with tump lines. The heaviest load went on my backpack board, the one I bought from Sears many years ago for hiking in the California Sierras. It was tricky keeping our balance as we waded across the river. I nearly slipped and fell. The men thanked me for the ride to town and I thanked them for their help with the cargo. I wondered if Maximo's new sandals rubbed blisters on his feet. And how did Pablo walk all that way with no shoes at all? His wife will be pleased with the new corn grinder.

One weekend, for a change of scenery, the three of us decided to go to Minatitlan, a colorful, bustling oil town near the ocean. Carrie and I rode a borrowed horse while Carl hiked alongside over the very muddy trail. By the time we reached our car in Soteapan our clothes were sopping wet and very muddy. We had failed to put our "town clothes" in a plastic bag inside the saddle bag. They got wet when we waded across the rivers but we put them on anyway and they dried just fine.

In Mina we filled two butane tanks for our stove at home

God's Talk

then stopped to eat lunch in a little open-air eating place in the market: fried fish, soup, tortillas and Spanish rice. While we were eating, some naughty boys pushed over a kettle of hot beans. It was balanced precariously on a charcoal burner. The feet and legs of two women working nearby were burned. I felt sorry for them.

I had hoped for a better trail trip on our way home. But alas, it was even worse than it had been earlier. It had rained just enough to muddy the trail. Someone loaned us a mule to carry the butane tanks strapped to its back. Carl walked alongside while Carrie and I rode the horse again. The horse gingerly picked his way down a particularly slippery slope. His hind legs went out from under him and I was afraid Carrie would slip off his back end into the mud and tumble down the steep incline. She was brave, though, and hung on to me for dear life. The horse slid a short distance down the hill before he could get all four feet under him again, and we continued cautiously on our way. Horses aren't as surefooted as mules are on a rocky, rugged, muddy trail like that.

Darkness had settled by the time we arrived at our house. What a bedraggled-looking threesome we were, exhausted and starving. I never could have imagined that a tiny little adobe hut in the middle of the jungle could look so inviting as ours did that night! We scurried around to light kerosene lamps so we could fix something to eat. The tomato soup, toasted cheese sandwiches and *cafe con leche* (coffee with milk) tasted extra good as more rain began to pound on the tin roof. How comfy it feels to be safe, warm and snug.

Rain, Rain, Rain

Carl tell about another trip:

On one of our monthly shopping trips four fellows from the village went with us. All the noise, hustle and bustle of big city traffic frightened them. The store clerks had little patience with their limited, mediocre Spanish. We parked across the street from the jail where the prisoners extended their arms out between the bars to greet people passing on the street who would stop and talk to them. The string hammocks which they made to sell were also hanging out between the bars, draped from poles fastened to the window frames. An unusual, colorful sight! Also, Acayucan is set right smack in the middle of the Pan-American Highway that goes from Texas to Panama. Sometimes we see American tourists wander the streets or eat at the sidewalk cafes.

We always enjoyed browsing at the only grocery store in town, Casa Iglesias, which was as close to a supermarket as one could find this far out in the tropics. We craved ice cream so before we left town, we each had a banana split at a place that looked clean. What a treat that was since we didn't have access to anything cold at home.

One year just before Christmas, Carl went to the Acayucan bus station to pick up our order of medicines, a barrel for collecting our water and a roll of plastic we had ordered from Mexico City. Also waiting there for us was a big Christmas box sent by a family at the English-speaking Union Church in Mexico City where we usually attended when we were in the City. How exciting! On Christmas day we opened the colorfully wrapped presents inside. There was a wide selection of edible goodies that were unavailable here: canned ham, pickles, maraschino cherries, candy, marshmallows, nuts, marmalade, canned corn, soup, tuna, peaches, peanut butter, deviled ham, soap, Kleenex, popcorn, cake

God's Talk

and brownie mixes, noodles, powdered sugar, raisins, baking chocolate, cookies. Such delightful surprises sparked up our lives at times like this. What thoughtful gifts from thoughtful, caring people.

Another trip was to have been our wedding anniversary outing to Lake Catemaco. As we started out with the red Ford, suddenly it wouldn't go forward. The transmission fluid had leaked out. Water had gotten in the transmission during the one and only time we had forded the river with it. We decided not to ford the river again until the bridges were completed. Since the car was discombobulated, we ended up going to Minatitlan instead, taking the third-class bus along with people, pigs, chickens and turkeys. After getting a few groceries, we found an ice cream shop and made that our anniversary treat.

Two hours later, lugging our purchases, we caught the last bus to Soteapan and hiked home by the silvery light of the moon and the jungle noises ringing in our ears. This all resulted in a workout rather than the relaxed outing we had planned. It was dark when we arrived at our car, so Carl waited until the next day to hike back to Soteapan and add the transmission fluid he bought in town.

It was raining heavily the morning the radio message came in from Mexico City telling us copies of the Gospel of Mark were fresh off the press and had been sent by bus to Acayucan where we could pick them up. We weren't about to let rain stop us from picking up the precious cargo. We quickly got ready and drove our carry-all to Acayucan. On our way to town, the Huasuntlan river hadn't yet become swollen so our Chevy carry-all forded it without incident. We had expected the books to arrive during the dry season so it was

Rain, Rain, Rain

ironic they finally got here when the road travel and river crossings were very uncertain.

While we were in town, though, it rained all day. When we reached the big river on the way back it was dark. We couldn't see that the rushing water was over a foot deeper than when we crossed earlier in the day. Carl decided to try crossing anyway. Not a good idea. In the middle of the river the motor began to cough, sputter, then died. There we sat-- with water pouring in over the floor boards and our vehicle moving gradually with the current. It was scary. Time to pray! We couldn't even move backwards out of the river. It was easy to imagine that the swift current might even carry us, our precious cargo and all downstream. Our first thought was to protect the boxes of Mark's Gospel from getting wet so we piled them on top of everything else in the carry-all.

Talk about feeling foolish! Eight young Aztec fellows watched us from the river bank--probably laughing and commenting on these crazy Americans stuck in the middle of the river. They graciously offered to push us back out of the river and up the river bank. Carl put the vehicle in neutral, let out the clutch, and with the fellows pushing us, the Chevy carry-all rolled back over the rocky river bottom and up the river bank to where the road led to the highway. After a short wait, the carry-all sputtered to life again.

Safe at last, thankful we weren't carried downstream, we drove the fifty miles back to Acayucan and stayed at the Hotel Plaza for the night. By 11:00 a.m. the next day, the rain had stopped, the sun was shining brightly and the river had receded to its normal level. This time we crossed without any problems. Whew! What an ordeal.

God's Talk

June 18, 1970 - Five-day Trail Trip

Carl describes the trip to other Aztec towns:

It was a gorgeous day for a trail trip. Partly cloudy. No threat of rain. We left at 7:45 a.m. with a burro loaded with medicines, our sleeping gear, including two foam mattresses and a hammock, 75 copies of the newly arrived Gospel of Mark, 60 copies of Acts, and 15 copies of the Old Testament stories, plus Spanish New Testaments and dictionaries. A big load for the burro, but not excessive. Amazing how much cargo a burro can carry if it's well balanced. Our faithful horse, King, was good for riding where it wasn't too steep or rocky. Carrie chose to walk barefooted like the village women do.

We headed northeast toward the gulf coast, through the pine woods on a mountainous trail we had never traveled before. Thankfully, our guide, Evaristo Martinez, knew the trail well. The fresh, pleasantly fragrant pines formed a welcome canopy from the hot sun. Perched on the summit of the ridge, we could look far off to the east and view the shimmering blue waters of our destination, the Gulf of Mexico. We knew that a hard two-day journey lay ahead of us.

The ridge ended abruptly in the pine woods where the trail descended sharply and wound through tangled jungle-type growth and a bamboo thicket. People were at work in their fields near the trail. Newly sprouted grass was poking up through the brown soil after being burned off during the dry season in preparation for planting crops. At a clear stream, we filled each of our canteens and added iodine solution to purify the water.

Rain, Rain, Rain

Climbing another three hours we were among pines trees again. People in the village of Encinal Amarillo gave us a polite, but guarded reception. We chatted with the village office manager and displayed our literature on a makeshift table under the trees. Later he invited us to eat with him and his family. He was the only person who bought anything from us--a ballpoint pen.

There had been very little if any exposure to the Gospel in these small Aztec towns along the coastal trail so most of the people were skeptical about why we were there. A group of men, women and children gathered around to see what these strangers who could talk their language were doing in their village! We read aloud from Mark's Gospel to several people. One little lady, who had never heard about the Jesús in the Bible (Jesús, pronounced hey-SOOS in Spanish, is a popular man's name in Mexico.), wondered <u>which</u> Jesús this was. Was it the Jesús over yonder who has a lot of children? Even though we explained this was God's Son, we got mostly blank expressions. It was after 4:00 p.m. when we left there.

A 45-minute hike brought us to the village of Ocotal. As we displayed the books, a small group of interested fellows gathered around us. One even encouraged others to buy. "It's good," he said. But nobody bought. They claimed they had no money. At this rate, we would carry lots of books back home with us. But, after all, this was our first such contact with these people. Also, people in these villages in the "outback" had no schools and could neither read nor write. We would need to come back again when we had Scripture Recordings available. Maybe we could manage to provide literacy classes, too.

Thirty or more families lived in each village. Hopefully, the next time we came, they will be less suspicious and our efforts would be more fruitful. The trip could easily be done in a day, or perhaps an overnight, in order to find more people at home. The town secretary offered us lodging in the "office," a small thatched hut near a large central plaza where we could hang our hammock and spread our mattresses for the night.

For our breakfast the next morning one of the ladies cooked eggs and patted tortillas. After boiling some water for a chocolate drink, we packed up and were on our way again. The trail passed through virgin jungle, lush and exotic as any National Geographic picture. We were surprised and excited to see monkeys swinging in the tree tops. We supposed they lived farther up in the mountains, but we were told they are often seen in large groups along this trail.

Other wild life we saw were squirrels, lizards, a tiny snake, a larger snake someone killed shortly before, and brightly colored butterflies in all their finery. The jungle bird songs echoed through the forests.

In several places the trail was blocked by trees that were slashed out of the jungle to make a new field. The "slash and burn" method of agriculture was still used extensively in the rural areas. Twice we had to use our machetes to clear a path through a tangle of jungle vines. No attempt had been made to keep the trail open for pack animals at these places.

This main trail to the Gulf of Mexico coast had some very steep and rocky inclines, but in only one or two places did we need to dismount--a precaution against the animal stumbling or falling. At one river crossing the large rocks were slippery and caused both horse and burro to stumble. We feared the cargo would get wet. Fortunately, the sure-footed burro caught his balance before the water reached the box of books. When I packed the cargo, I had decided not to put them in water-proof

Rain, Rain, Rain

bags because there was no sign of rain. I didn't think of river crossings--we live and learn.

The second day on the trail we took turns riding and walking and ate lunch at a pretty spot where two streams joined. There we bathed, rested and cooked our chicken and rice soup over a small open fire. Late in the afternoon, we arrived tired and footsore at the Aztec town of La Valentina. A former resident of Mecayapan had settled there several years before, and he kindly offered us lodging in the loft at his house. We gladly accepted not knowing we would have to battle fleas and bedbugs all night! Our books created only mild interest because, here again, few could read and write. At least we introduced them to written materials.

The next day we trudged on to two more villages on the coast, Pilapillo and Pajapan. We didn't draw the usual crowd at either one but instead went to individual homes. We were pleasantly surprised to get warm, friendly receptions. Someone had warned us that the Gospel might not be welcome there. Carl announced to the few gathered around that the Catholic priest of this parish had bought copies of all our books and was encouraging people to read God's Word. Then the Gospel of Mark and book of Acts sold like hotcakes! There is a school in Pajapan so most of the younger people could read.

The Pajapan dialect is significantly different from the Mecayapan dialect, but in spite of that difference, people bought the books. We discovered a small group of Christians that met each night for services. They asked if we would translate Scripture in their dialect. The leaders offered to help us, so we arranged to come over at another time and work with them on the translation. (The details of that effort are written in the section titled Translation Work in Pajapan, *pg 127*)

God's Talk

We passed through the town of Tatahuicapan where we met a few people but didn't linger since we were nearly out of the books we had brought with us.

Summary

People in the first four towns appeared anemic and lethargic. In contrast, we saw noticeable differences in Pajapan and Tatahuicapan. People were more alert and healthy, had bustling communities, thriving schools and were accessible by roads in dry weather. Accepting the hospitality of the people was a real privilege. They gave us their best in every way, generously served us eggs, tortillas and coffee. Meat was served only once, and that was *tepescuintle*, a wild animal with delicious tasting meat. Meat went a **long** way when each person was given two or three small pieces of meat in lots of broth along with a big stack of fresh hot tortillas to eat it with. No one served us black beans, though; they don't produce well in that sandy soil. The men there hunt and fish since they are close to the Gulf.

We slept on saplings lashed together, straw mats on dirt floors, hammocks and, in the more prosperous villages, on cots. Can't say we made friends with all the creepie-crawlies, though--mosquitoes, fleas, bedbugs, cockroaches and gnats. We arrived home very bitten and constantly scratching. Such things passed, however, and we were none the worse for it. It was more than worth it to have contact with the rest of the people who speak the Isthmus Nahuatl dialect.

Nine-year-old Carrie kept right up with us, skipping happily along barefooted, fascinated with the abundant wild life in the jungle. When we got back, as Carl and I were nursing aching muscles, she said in all seriousness "I'm ready to go again!" Ah, the sweet resiliency of youth....

Observations of the Trail Trip

- There was a myriad of fleas where we slept in the *topanco* (loft) overnight.
- Carrie walked barefoot the whole 50 miles round trip.
- Carl and Carrie challenged each other up the big long hill.
- Cockroaches crawled out of the tortilla bowl at our host's house.
- Carl left a record player and set of records in Pilapillo.
- We heard the differences in the Pajapan Nahuatl dialect.
- We plan to go back and work on translation.
- At one place we were suspected of practicing magic because we could speak their language.
- At the beach Carrie caught crabs, and a lady cooked them for us. Delicious!
- We ate freshly caught fish. Didn't get any *chacalin* (shrimp) though.
- First thing we were offered at one place was fresh coconut milk. Mmmm!
- We slept in the newly built school room in Pajapan.
- We slept in our own hammocks where we could hang them
- We swam in the warm Gulf waters

God's Talk

Roads, Bridges and Other Improvements

Fall of 1972

Carl tells of plans for a road to Mecayapan:

We listened to the rumble of machinery in the distance as the road graders came closer and closer. It was the talk of the town. What a difference to have a real graded road to Mecayapan! The road and three bridges are scheduled to be finished in six months. The new road snakes its way through the tropical vegetation and is far enough along for trucks to use now.

The government surveyors laid out a street plan in Mecayapan for fully graded, but unpaved streets to form an area the size of a large city block. The machinery graded the streets right down through the helter-skelter arrangement of huts--a hodge-podge of thatch-roofed houses set in all directions. Ten or twelve houses had to be moved in the process. It will soon look very different around here. Wait until the next rain washes huge ruts and gullies down the streets! Concrete sidewalks and *curbs were also in the plan. I'll believe it when I see it. Imagine this primitive Indian village having "streets" alongside thatched roofed huts and adobe or split-pole walls.*

All this activity means outside contacts will come in that will greatly influence this economy and culture. What changes loom ahead for these isolated pockets of people tucked back in the mountains who, up to now, have been secluded and steeped in their centuries-old traditions? The Bible in their own language can be a tremendous stabilizing influence. With God's help, we will work diligently to that end.

January 23, 1973

The big, beautiful (to us!) bridge was **finally** completed over the river we had crossed on foot or forded all these years. With great rejoicing we drove our car over it on our way to the village this time. The children in the schoolrooms across the plaza whooped and hollered with welcoming yells as they leaned out the open windows to watch us drive the red Ford to our house for the first time. After school they came to admire this new phenomena. They rubbed their grimy little hands all over it so Carl gave them rags and they took turns wiping the dust off. The shiny red car looked incongruous next to a mud-walled house, but finally we had a wonderfully convenient access to the paved highway and outside world. Roads make such a difference to a culture. Those ten miles of dirt road were graveled and eventually became an all-weather road into our town. In time, this whole mountainous area would be open to the outside world.

Many other changes were coming to this once-isolated area. Having a road meant that second-class bus service was established into Mecayapan. The people could market their produce much easier and perhaps increase their yearly income. The stores and taverns expanded their inventory.

Public School

On our arrival in 1965, we had full view from our front door of the newly-built concrete-block school building across the plaza. A national holiday with annual celebration programs and parties marked the end of the school term. The term had begun November 20 and ended February 1.

There were four male Spanish-speaking teachers with about 50 pupils, kindergarten through sixth grade. Six large classrooms were built in a U-shape around a grassy courtyard. A generator for electricity and diesel pump for two flush toilets were used only on special occasions. They were often nonfunctional. When a doctor came in 1972, he set up his clinic in one of the empty school rooms.

Carrie had begged to go to the school ever since we arrived, so she was invited to go and listen to the lessons in Spanish with the other kindergartners. Something happened at school that first day that caused her to not want to go back. "It's too hard," she said. She reported that some of the older boys splashed her with muddy water, and the teacher spanked them all for it! From that time on, she was satisfied to stay home and never asked to go again. I soon began home-schooling her.

Mid-morning snack of fresh-baked bread and milk was furnished. The man who operated the corn grinding machine baked the bread in the large mud oven next door to us. He used flour, milk and butter provided by the Mexican

God's Talk

government that came from U.S. surplus. The children were instructed to bring their own cups for chocolate milk, also from U.S. surplus. It was interesting how they reacted to this innovation. Their custom was to take home any food that was given to them rather than eat it there so they could share it with the rest of the family. The teachers allowed them to do that instead of trying to change the custom.

After we put up a pencil-sharpener on the porch, the school children were attracted more than ever to our house. We were surprised the school didn't have a pencil-sharpener as standard equipment. They flocked to our house to use it on their way to school and at recess times. Considering the language barrier they had to overcome, they learned to read and write quite well,. They liked it when we invited them to read to us from the books on our display table. It was a joy to learn to know the future adults of the village.

The Spanish-speaking teachers were young, vivacious "pioneers." We had good Spanish practice when they came to our house for coffee, cookies and a visit in the evenings. They said they wanted to learn some English and arranged to come over on Saturday mornings, but they never showed up. Three teachers helped us proof-read the Spanish version of the Health Book we were working on. It was a very interesting three-hour visit. They expressed appreciation for our efforts to get helpful information across to the people in their own language. One evening we invited them over for hamburgers, french fries, Koolaid and chocolate cake, which they ate with gusto. They were delighted to have a typical American meal and thanked us profusely.

Another time we asked for their help in wording the Spanish introduction for a small booklet Carl had been working on. They followed his suggestion that they use it in their classes to instill a feeling of pride in the Nahuatl language instead of inferiority so the children could see that their language was on the same level as any other language.

Water Sources

Much of our daily life in the village revolved around obtaining a reliable supply of clean drinking water. During our first couple of years we had only two sources, rainwater runoff from the roof into a barrel during the rainy season or water hauled in metal buckets or clay pots from the river. Either way, we purified it by one of two ways: boiled it for ten minutes or added chlorine tablets or a small amount of saturated iodine solution made with iodine crystals. Kool Aid, fresh orange or lemon juice masked the medicinal taste quite well.

In this climate there are only two seasons: wet and dry. Daily drenching rains from May to November gave us abundant drinking water from the galvanized metal roof. The runoff drained into the roof gutters and down the spout to a 50-gallon barrel at the outside corner of the house. If we caught a supply in containers directly from the gutter, we didn't have to boil it or treat it with iodine. Also, our neighbor girl didn't need to balance a heavy bucket of water on her head as she trudged up the steep hill from the water hole carved out of the river bank.

In 1970 the state government of Veracruz, as one of the community improvement projects, constructed a water tower on the hill above the town and then a concrete dam on the river that bordered the town, and a diesel engine was installed. This meant expensive diesel fuel had to be used to pump water <u>up</u> to the tower. Clean (?) water was intended to flow

God's Talk

down into a network of pipelines leading to public faucets placed several yards apart throughout the village. In the center of town a laundry/bath house was built with flush toilets. With all this modernization, everyone expected a steady supply of running water in the faucets.

But, alas! There were at least two BIG problems. The diesel pump was located downstream where people bathed, washed their corn, laundered their clothes, crossed the stream with their animals, and allowed their pigs to wallow. This amount of contamination made it unsuitable for drinking water. We noted a marked increase in intestinal infestations after this so-called "improvement" of installing the pump.

After the diesel pump was installed, it broke down frequently, and the town authorities didn't have the tools, money or know-how to make repairs, drain the engine oil or fix a faucet when needed! A couple of times, Carl was consulted about what could be done to fix it. He knew how to fix a lot of things, but this was way out of his expertise. Consequently, the pump was out of commission more often than not. If the pump didn't work, the water tower stood empty and totally useless. People stoically reverted to doing what they had always done and carried water by hand or on their heads from the river. As luck would have it, a year later the pump was rendered completely and forever inoperable when, during a particularly heavy rainstorm, the dam broke and the pump was washed down the river by the watery deluge!

Roads, Bridges and Other Improvements

Carl laments the water problems:

Today the water in the pipes is all gone, <u>again</u>--the usual motor trouble. Why can't they get it started? I'm frustrated! I think the heat and everything else is getting to me. The last week was really hot with no sign of rain and our water barrels are nearly empty. There is a free-flowing spring at the bottom of the hill with water that is relatively safe to drink without boiling. The downside is that we have to carry it up the steep hill in a bucket. It tastes better, though. Finally, last night, after two weeks without rain, we had about an inch, partially filling one barrel. I caught enough roof-water to fill our jugs.

In October 1971, a few days after we returned from a year's furlough, the town authorities came around to ask me if I would help them build a water system that would flow by gravity from a stream nearly a mile up the hill at the edge of town. John Lind and the Popolucas had built a water system like that a year before in the neighboring village of Ocotal Chico. The people in Mecayapan saw how well it worked so they desperately wanted one too. I agreed to explore the issue further.

*Dick Bronson, one of our Wycliffe engineers, was willing to spend several days with us in the village. He looked over the situation, drew up a design for a dam and calculated the size of pipe and other supplies needed for the number of potential users. He also designed a sand filter to purify the water for drinking. Best of all, his design did not--I repeat, did **not**--require any mechanical equipment that would need repairs! This is just what was needed--a <u>simple</u> water system for people not yet technology-literate. This system would eliminate the constant unsuccessful struggle to repair the unreliable diesel pump.*

This project required a lot of my time that otherwise would have been spent at the translation desk, but I knew it was also important to contribute to the community and make a difference in this way. It was gratifying to see how the townspeople invested themselves and their money and took ownership of this project.

The translation program was on hold for about three months while Carl supervised the work crews, worked alongside the men and kept the financial records straight. Two hundred heads of families (40% of the townspeople) paid their assessment dues to help cover cost of materials and also were expected to regularly give time to the project.

January 1972

Carl writes about the water project:

The water project is in full swing now. Our aim is to provide accessible, clean drinking water and hopefully lower incidences of intestinal parasites. The town authorities called a town meeting and explained the plan to the people. A small dam would be constructed about a mile up the hill at the headwaters of the stream that flows through the village, far enough outside of town so that people would not be contaminating it, thus giving a purer source of water.

The stream was temporarily diverted while the dam was constructed. The men cleared one-half mile of dense jungle growth for an access road to haul in materials. They moved large rocks and dug a ditch for the pipeline nearly 900 yards uphill from the water tower to where a spring-fed stream burbled happily over the stones. A concrete collection tank was built for the water filter. Sand and gravel were sifted into several sizes to be used in different levels. First a layer of large rocks, then smaller rocks, large gravel, small gravel, coarse, medium and fine sand

Roads, Bridges and Other Improvements

in that order. A top layer of large stones was then placed on the fine sand to keep it from being washed away by heavy rains.

A one-inch pipe was laid down in the hand-dug ditch to carry the water by gravity at the rate of nine gallons a minute into the 12,500 gallon water tower/storage tank that had been erected by the government. Forty water faucets connected to the network of pipes from the water tower had already been placed all over town so most families could have a faucet close to their huts. The plan was for more faucets to be added as people could afford them.

The completion of the water project in the spring of 1972 was the culmination of many hours of hand labor. *(Note: this system is still in use as of this writing 37 years later.)*

Alas! Several months after completion of the dam, one of the heaviest rain storms in people's memory messed up the filtering system at the dam. Oh dear, after all that sweat and labor. But, voilá! The next day a group of men were hard at work repairing the sand filter. This proved to us that they were taking ownership of the whole project. We felt confident they would carry on into the future even after we left it. It wasn't long until Aztecs in another village wanted Carl to do the same thing for them. That had to be put on hold so translation could move ahead. Many community projects could take our time, but we had to set our own priorities.

Even though translation was delayed, the water project was a worthwhile interruption and our expectations were fulfilled. It gave us unusual opportunities to work alongside the people and meet a felt need in the community. The convenience of having plenty of clear, pure water gush out at the flick of a faucet was a beautiful miracle and such a blessing to people. It helped reduce the incidence of intestinal parasites and other water-borne diseases.

By now the people realized that we had not gone there for our own personal gain, but to help where we could. As fresh clean water flowed into the town system, we trusted that the people would have a thirst for the Water of Life, God's Word in their own language.

Electricity Comes to Town

November 1972 - Carl writes about electricity coming:

The Mecayapan townspeople, with government help, worked hard to bring electric lines over the rugged jungle terrain. Five months later the light poles were in place, the power lines tightened and light fixtures installed. Electricity was ready to be switched on in Mecayapan.

With the recently completed bridges and roads, and now with electricity, the outside world has opened up even more for these once isolated, mountainous areas. Street lights and electric lights in the grass-thatched huts give the town a whole different personality. With adequate lighting at night people are able to read more when they come in from their field work. Our house was wired with electricity, too, so we enclosed our porch to make a library/reading room/book store where people could read, check out, or buy books.

Electricity brought one big change that we didn't anticipate though--a huge increase in loud music played over the loudspeakers of the cantinas (beer joints) scattered around the village so the whole town could "enjoy" it. Previously, the cantinas used only battery-operated record players. When the batteries gave out, so did the music.

Now, with 24/7 electricity available, the raucous, intrusive music didn't stop. Sometimes it was blasted around town from the roofs of two or three different cantinas simultaneously. With that many going at a time it really made for sound pollution. Music started early in the morning and often was going at intervals all through the day and night. Requests for special music to honor someone's birthday were announced over the loudspeakers, too. Some love-sick fellow would sing off key to his girlfriend. Intoxicated men made long involved speeches with slurred voices out over the airwaves.

Carrie and I tried to keep her school lessons going in spite of the pervasive noise that made it so hard to concentrate. It was even harder for the Scripture translation team to concentrate. We began to wish for the more tranquil days and nights before the trappings of so-called civilization spoiled the ambience.

Gospel Recordings

Records were a powerful tool of evangelism for a pre-literate people, and the Christians were looking forward to the wide ministry these would have in the scattered villages of this dialect area, including the Christians in Pajapan. Several local Christians worked with Carl in April 1967 preparing the scripts for Gospel Recordings technicians who were scheduled to come to Mecayapan to make recordings of the Gospel songs, Scriptures and Bible Stories that were newly-translated.

Jim Middlestedt, who was in charge of making the records,

God's Talk

informed us later that his trip to Pajapan to get recordings in that dialect was very successful.

Jim writes about the recordings:

> "The folks there understood about 98% of the texts recorded in Mecayapan and were thrilled by them. They recorded stories of the Creation and The Fall, The Death and Resurrection of Jesus and two original Aztec songs. Pajapan has some real contrasts to Mecayapan. It is covered with beautiful grass and there are about 30 stores. Every family has its own pozo (water hole), each a little room carved into the bank of the stream with a manantial (spring) for drinking water, one for bathing, and one for washing clothes. Hope you can get there soon. The brethren would be thrilled to have you come. We are counting on you to take the records over there. We also went to Ixhuatlan del Sureste, but people there 35 or younger don't speak Nahuatl anymore. The older people understood about 98% of Pajapan's dialect and about 96% of Mecayapan's. Thanks for taking such good care of us."

By the end of the summer Gospel Recordings sent us a set of six records, four in the Mecayapan dialect and two in the Pajapan dialect, along with a good quality transistorized record player. These were wonderful assets for sharing Scriptures and songs. Evening visitors listened attentively to the records and practiced reading the new booklets.

Aztec Young People Squeezed between Two Cultures

In the early 1970's, "Tribes in Transition" was a good description of what was happening in many tribal areas where translation teams worked. A certain percentage of indigenous young people seemed to be ready for some changes

Roads, Bridges and Other Improvements

in their socio-economic standards as they had more frequent contact with the national culture in the outside world. For some, it was confusing and bewildering to adjust to the changes that came flooding in along with roads and electricity. Before many months passed, several thatched-roof houses sprouted TV antennas!

Our friend Lucio weathered the changes with less trauma. After he helped us at our first linguistic workshop, he worked as a mechanic in Mexico City. We hoped he could resist the inevitable pull to the larger national culture at the risk of abandoning his own culture, his birthright. For him and other Aztec young people, more conflicting emotional struggles are sure to come. Hopefully the Scriptures will be able to bridge that gap and provide a stabilizing influence.

When Genaro came back to the village he had a hard time maintaining his Christian testimony. He had serious feelings of rebellion and inner conflicts against his own culture. Having tasted the outside world, for awhile he became restless and discontented. Other young people too, caught in the squeeze between two distinct cultures, faced unique problems. It was our concern that the Christians especially be able to survive it as children of God. He could help them withstand the onslaught of modern civilization as it began to creep in and replace their traditional ways of living.

The Mexican government took a bold step when the Department of Education fully endorsed and financed bilingual education. It was truly heartening to those of us working in the various language areas. Use of the indigenous languages was actively encouraged as well as learning Spanish. Quite a few Aztec young people from our area have gone on for government-sponsored higher education and bilingual teacher training certification. With diploma in hand, they are

God's Talk

now qualified to teach their own people while at the same time preserving their own language and culture.

Family Holiday Times

Christmas 1965

As we approached our first Christmas in Mexico, we battled nostalgia, homesickness and loneliness. Nothing could replace holiday times with family and friends. The short-wave radio brought us Christmas music when we had time to listen. We hiked up to the pine forest and chose a small pine tree to take home and decorate with hand-made paper chains, popcorn strings, aluminum foil balls and icicles. We added colorful plastic salt and pepper shakers that were premiums in cereal boxes. They vaguely resembled Christmas decorations. Then we topped the whole thing with a foil-covered cardboard star. Christmas cards, greetings and gifts from many of our friends arrived in time to open before Christmas. These all helped to assuage our yearning to be with family.

Our spirits lifted tremendously when we were invited to spend the weekend at the home of an American couple, Bert and Jean Fairweather, Baptist missionaries living in Acayu-

God's Talk

can. After four months of stumbling over every other word in Nahuatl, I was <u>so</u> weary and <u>so</u> ready to speak English with someone besides Carrie or Carl.

However, the week before Christmas Carl became very sick with fever, diarrhea and vomiting and was in bed for several days. I diagnosed it as typhoid so I medicated him with Chloromycetin, and he quickly improved. He wasn't sure, though, if he would feel like dragging himself over the trail to spend the weekend with Fairweathers. If not, we could expect to spend a rather dreary weekend just looking at each other and the village people.

Although Carl's illness delayed us by one day, our plans worked out after all. Christmas morning Carrie and I rode the mule, and Carl felt well enough to ride the horse that Pastor John loaned us. Jose went along to bring the animals back. Even in his weakened condition Carl tolerated the 90 minute trail ride by pushing himself to the limit. He was longing for contact with American friends, too!

We joined the Fairweathers, three Americans who operated an orphanage for abandoned Mexican children outside Acayucan, and Norm Nordell, a fellow WBT member. The group was just sitting down to dinner when we arrived. Eight adults and three children gathered around a lace-covered table loaded with an array of typical American holiday foods, decorated very attractively with candles and a centerpiece. The beauty and food soothed our starved souls after living in the starkly primitive village conditions. Everything tasted absolutely scrumptious and delectable! I was amazed that Carl felt like eating after such an intestinal upset. But apparently he tolerated it well with no harm done. This was the perfect way to celebrate the holiday--to relax, chatter in English, eat familiar, delicious food and reflect on the meaning of the season.

Carrie and the two Fairweather girls had a great time playing together. She enjoyed playmates with whom she could freely converse, too. It was a morale booster to all of us, for sure. Sunday we attended the chapel where Fairweathers held services in Spanish. Monday we did more visiting at their home. Tuesday evening we returned home over the trail, carrying with us pleasant memories.

Christmas 1966

It was a chilly, rainy day in Mecayapan, so with a crackling fire going in the fireplace all day, we invited visitors in to warm themselves and chat awhile. The blustery storm from the north brought a cold front (55 degrees) and it started to rain again so no one came that evening. We were happy for the chance to spend quiet family time opening our gifts. Carrie was so excited she could hardly wait another minute to play her three new records.

Christmas 1967

We spent a very simple but satisfying Christmas in the village. We made our own little tree out of Spanish moss, decorated it with popcorn and handmade tinfoil decorations. Our handmade manger scene attracted lots of visitors and was a wonderful way to talk about Jesus and His birth and show off the brand-new Christmas story book in Nahuatl. Some people, especially the men, had heard the Christmas story in Spanish but didn't understand all the words. We translated a whole phrase that came out like this, *"She laid Him in the box where the animals eat because there was no room for them in the house where people sleep."*

God's Talk

We used colorful Christmas cards from the year before to make covers for 250 copies of the Christmas Story booklets that we would read aloud to people when they visited. Some copies went to each of the four groups of believers with the hope that each copy would have a special ministry. We detected people's growing pride in the printed language as well as their ability to read it. Since the school had begun three years before, at least one person per family could read some Spanish. As time went on, we taught more native language reading classes.

Reading Nahuatl was difficult at first even for those who could read Spanish, but they caught on quickly since we used the same Spanish letters for the Nahuatl alphabet. That year we were thoroughly contented among our beloved Aztec friends!

Christmas 1968

We celebrated Christmas at the Ixmi workshop center. The main event was delicious barbecued goat meat prepared by the Otomi language helpers. As was their custom, the Otomis dug a shallow pit, wrapped chunks of goat meat in maguey leaves, laid them over hot stones in the pit, thoroughly insulated them by covering them with more maguey leaves and baked them for two hours. Then each language team shared favorite carry-in side dishes and joined in Christmas carol singing in Spanish.

Christmas 1971

This year was different for us. We brought back 70 pounds of ice when we shopped in Acayucan. Then, with our one gallon hand-crank freezer that we brought back after furlough, we made four batches of ice cream and served ice cream cones to 125 people! We could have made four more batches if we hadn't run out of ice. It was a real treat for our friends in the village who rarely got to taste anything cold unless they bought a cold soft drink in a town on the highway.

Christmas 1973

Our Wycliffe friends Al and Delores Rice, along with their two sons, Mike and Chris, spent five wonderful days with us in the village. They wanted to get away from the high altitude, smog and cold weather in Mexico City where they lived and worked at the headquarters. Again, the chance to talk English with someone besides ourselves was so very welcome! All of us hiked up the mountain to choose a pretty Christmas tree. Together we baked goodies and put last minute touches on homemade gifts.

Delores and I walked through the town looking for a turkey to buy, but no one was willing to sell us one, so we bought two chickens instead. For dessert, I served mincemeat pies with homemade ice cream for Christmas dinner. That's about as American as you can get in the jungles. On cool evenings we sat by the fireplace and shared stories about Christmases past. No worries about the energy crisis there where firewood is plentiful.

The only visible reminder we had of the approaching Christmas holiday were three beautiful eight-foot tall poinsettia plants in the corner of our yard with thirty huge red blooms. The daytime temperature hovered in the 70's and 80's so sleeveless dresses and T-shirts were comfortable. The day after Christmas we took a lunch to the beach where the children loved to splash around in the warm Gulf waters. After such fun together, we were sorry to see them leave and return to the City.

Thanksgiving

One year we spent Thanksgiving with other Wycliffe colleagues: Linds, Larry and Nancy Clark, and Betty Herr. Again our gracious hosts were Bert and Jean Fairweather. What a grand time we had. And such delicious food. Roast turkey with giblet gravy, ham, stuffing, mashed potatoes, green beans with mushroom sauce, baked corn, pineapple in lime jello, fresh cranberry relish, cranberry jelly, homemade rolls, wild grape jelly, iced tea or Koolaid, chocolate swirl pound cake, three kinds of pie: apple, mince, and my specialty--shoo-fly. This meal couldn't have been surpassed anywhere in the States!

The nine children had a great time. The women chatted around the table while the men had their conversation in the living room. Friday morning we all went shopping in Coatzacoalcos, ate a picnic lunch at the beach and let the warm Gulf water lap gently around our feet. Not the typical winter holiday activity in the U.S., but oh such fun.

Easter

One Easter morning we skipped away by ourselves for the day and relaxed in the fragrant pine forest high above the town. We swung in our three Yucatecan-style string hammocks hung from the lower branches of the pine trees. It was so restful to let the balmy breezes cool us as we swung gently and allowed the tension to drain out of our bodies. We had family devotions there, too, and quietly contemplated the meaning of the day.

This lovely family excursion included an Easter egg hunt with a dozen dyed hardboiled eggs. We took turns hiding them in the soft, thick, green grass. Carrie wanted us to hide them over again and again. She got such a big kick out of hunting them that we hid them at least ten times!

God's Talk

Mexico City and Beyond

Contacts with Mexican Christians

In Mexico City encouraging things were happening! Ten Christian professional Mexican young people had enrolled in the two-week linguistics courses taught in Spanish at the SIL Center. This was followed by two weeks of "mini jungle camp" training in the remote parts of their own country. We were thrilled by their reports about how they were profoundly touched and impressed with the taste of missionary life they received.

Several followed through and applied for membership with Wycliffe Bible Translators. They shared their enthusiasm and experiences at the Mexican Presbyterian church the next Sunday evening! It was evident that they were searching for answers to many of the same questions other young people were asking, "Why am I here? What is the point of the money-making merry-go-round we are in? How can I make my life really count for something?"

God's Talk

Mexico City Headquarters

As a partner with Wycliffe, our field work and academic arm was through the Summer Institute of Linguistics (SIL). In Spanish it is Instituto Linguistico de Verano, or ILV. The ILV Center was located in Tlalpan, a suburb of Mexico City. The entire five-acre property was completely enclosed by the customary (in Mexican cities) eight-foot high stone walls. Within the walls were motel-type rooms for those of us who came to the City from our villages, rooms for language helpers and modest apartments for permanent center staff. These buildings surrounded a large grassy area where the children could frolic, and adults could relax with an exciting, fast-paced volleyball game. Meals were served in a huge dining/kitchen area that could accommodate up to 150 people at a time. A comfortable lounge area with a fireplace lent an ambience where conversation groups could hang out. The Publications Department, a large auditorium and offices completed the campus complex.

The Center was always a beehive of activity. Teams came for R & R, to work on language projects, to take care of government papers, purchase supplies, renew driver's permits, get items from storage units or arrange for a consultant to supervise the progress of their publications. Usually after a workshop, we spent time there preparing our linguistic and/or translation projects for publication.

Sunday evenings we met in the spacious auditorium where we were inspired by reports given by translation teams that had come from their village locations. Cameron Townsend ("Uncle Cam"), the founder of WBT, and his wife Elaine often stopped in to report on their trips. They took one through Russia with a vision of preparing teams to translate the Bible for people groups in the Caucasus and Siberia. We heard exciting reports such as: 300 new members being accepted one year; U.S. Congressman Fred Harris introduced a bill proclaiming September 18 as National Bible Translation day; Rachel Saint and two Auca Christians from Ecuador attended the World Congress of Evangelism in West Berlin.

Branch Conference

Every two years a refreshing and stimulating two-week-long Branch Conference was held for the entire Mexico Branch membership. In the business sessions the group discussed and prayed together for many aspects of the work, but especially that the working relationships with the Mexican government would continue to be cordial.

Reports from each tribal area and department head reminded us of how God was working all over Mexico. New Testaments were in the works with more scheduled to be completed. The new computer and editing system greatly speeded up the tedious stages of proofreading manuscripts.

While we were in business sessions, Carrie spent time with other children in the well organized and supervised youth program.

Group Service

Sufficient support personnel was often in short supply at the Center, and at the workshop locations: Ixmiquilpan and Oaxaca. Then the backlog of materials waiting for typists and paste-up people to prepare literature for the Indian people groups would become too large. Translators were often asked to fill temporary group assignments to reduce the accumulated work load. Group service took time away from their translation work, but everyone willingly pitched in as needed.

In the summer of 1967, we took time out to accept a group service assignment. Carl taught Phonology and Phonetics in the summer linguistic courses at the University of Oklahoma in Norman. I served as hostess to students and staff. Carrie was cared for in the children's program. Students came for classes from 13 foreign countries, India, Germany Australia, Japan, Guatemala, to name a few.

In 1968 we agreed to help with the backlog in the publications department at headquarters in Mexico City. Carl did the layout work on New Testaments and other publications. I did paste-up related to printing and mailing out the prayer letters members sent to their donors. Both were demanding jobs, but it was rewarding to see Scripture portions in many languages coming off the presses faster as a result of our work.

(Ed. note: Before updated electronic equipment was installed in Mexico City, it literally took months and years of typing, proofreading, and re-typing before the final manuscript of the New Testaments could be handed in for publication.)

That Christmas, even though we would have liked to have been with our Aztec friends, admittedly it was pleasant to live in a comfortable apartment graced by a lovely Christmas tree from Canada, provided by a kind friend. My parents were visiting us that year, which made it extra special.

Mexico City and Beyond

Dialect Survey

In 1968 Carl went on an Aztec dialect survey with another Mexico branch member, Dave Persons. The purpose of this survey was to determine what differences there were in several of the regional Nahuatl dialects spoken in villages over a wide area of southern Veracruz. This w ould help us know how far the Scriptures in the Mecayapan dialect would be understood and what adaptations might be needed. Carrie and I remained at the Tlalpan Center during the four weeks they were gone.

Carl kept a detailed log of their experiences and encounters. A summary of it is included here:

From March 5 to March 30 Dave and Carl either drove Dave's four wheel drive or hiked to Aztec villages all over southern Veracruz. They encountered dust storms on the high plateau and drove through pretty country with lots of orchards and potato fields. They were received in thee villages they visited in a variety of ways that ranged from indifferent, silent and suspicious to friendly and hospitable.

They recorded word lists at various places so they could compare the different levels of intelligibility. They persuaded people to tell stories so they could analyze just how far a dialect would be understood.

They managed to get a story from one young fellow, but in general, it was only the old people who still spoke Nahuatl. They asked a taxi driver to take them to an old gentleman, Benito, who they were told <u>might</u> still know some of the language. They said he would be back the next day. Benito didn't show up so they went out to the country and talked to several other people.

They met Vicente, but he said he had no time to help. They trekked down to Xoteapan 10 minutes away with a population of 300 families. The town secretary was asleep. When he woke up, he agreed to help them on the word list and did some recording. And so it went.

They encountered lots of mosquitoes. One bit Carl on the lip. In Pajapan, Doña Francisca fed them so they didn't get hungry, bless her. She only started fixing the meal when they got there. They decided to take something to do while waiting. Work went slow a lot of the time. It was hard to get people to listen and cooperate.

Carl comments on results of survey:

> *In the middle of the night a man came calling for Señor Felix, in whose house we were sleeping. I told him he was sleeping out in the kitchen. In the morning Felix told us that it was someone wanting him to go help make a casket.*

> *The back room of Señor Felix's house has a dirt floor of nice, smooth sandy dirt. Both mornings the lady put a basin on this floor for us to wash our faces. The custom is you're not to get the water in the basin dirty, so you dip it out with one hand and let it drip on the floor as you wash your face. It helps keeps the dust down. I even washed under my arms that way. Bending over lets me do it without getting my trousers wet. I shaved by the big barber mirror but without cleaning the razor well afterward so as not to get the water dirty in the basin.*

Then a duck waddles in and drinks from the basin, leaving dirt in the water! Dave didn't wash his face this morning.

There are two areas in which a bilingualism test would be most helpful in determining the need for materials in Nahuatl. I wonder if this type of a test would show relative levels of comprehension in Spanish and Nahuatl.

The Nahuatl dialect survey was a worthwhile thing for me because it gives me a good idea of the extent to which the language is used in areas where we knew there were Aztecs, but that was about all we knew. The testing results and data collected will of course help determine our approach to the people in those areas where the language is still used extensively.

God's Talk

Furlough in the States

Carl writes about starting furlough:

We closed our village house July 3, 1970, and left for the States. It had rained every day for a week which meant the rivers would be high. We crossed the rising river in between rains and after it had receded, but the Chevy carry-all got stuck on the slippery climb up the bank from the river. A cargo truck came by and the kind driver pulled us up the rest of the way.

As I write this, we are enjoying the relaxation and beauty of Motel Posada Loma's flowering gardens at the base of majestic snow-covered Mount Orizaba. The rooms all have a view of the mountain, are tastefully decorated, and the food is served so attractively. The sun is shining, Marilyn and Carrie are swimming in the sparkling clean pool while I sit on a glider, write in this journal and play the guitar. This quiet, serene atmosphere

> *is very soothing to the spirit after coming from a hectic schedule. It will fortify us for the adjustments ahead of us.*

Our furlough plans included completing my degree in nursing at my alma mater, Messiah College in Pennsylvania, tutoring in Greek for Carl to help him do good translation work, and Carrie, now a fourth grader, entering public school for the first time. We rented a cute, unfurnished two-story white frame house in the small college town of Grantham. Friends loaned us furniture and supplies for the house. For me, going back to college after 20 years was a "mind-bending" experience! The social, intellectual and spiritual environment was very stimulating to all of us. Interaction with long-time friends boosted our spirits, and we needed all the boost we could get.

Settling into small-town America after primitive living in the jungle was quite a daunting task. Carrie was active in the Pioneer Girls group, took the significant step of accepting Christ as her Savior and was baptized at the Grantham church. Carl dipped into the Greek classes at Messiah and had official and personal speaking engagements in churches to present the work of Bible Translation. And, something he had always wanted to do, he took violin lessons from John Eaken, a well-known violinist. After only a few lessons, he fell and broke his left wrist while ice skating on the pond behind our house. He had a cast on it so that hampered his violin playing for awhile. I studied furiously and graduated with my Bachelor's Degree in Nursing in May 1971.

Furlough in the States

Counseling

In November 1972, John Lind, our supervisor of field programs, had a long visit with us. Carl shared his growing discouragement with parts of our program. John listened carefully and later wrote a sensitive, perceptive letter encouraging Carl to forge ahead. However, the enormity of everything that was expected and needed to be done overwhelmed and took its toll on him. He became increasingly distressed to the point that both our work and personal relationship were severely affected.

After the trauma related to Silvia's death in the spring of 1973, we consulted with our director Frank Robbins, and he recommended that, for our own emotional health, we needed some time for ourselves. We drove to southern California where Wycliffe had a Counseling Center. This provided the support we needed. Some Wycliffe friends generously offered their home to us while they were away for the summer. In the counseling sessions, we sorted out some of the recent traumatic experiences that had contributed to added stress. It was wonderful to rest and revitalize our spirits in a comfortable environment.

Back in the village in the fall, even with the counseling, our personal problems continued to trouble us. Our director advised us to do what we felt would be in our family's best interest. It was a difficult choice to think of interrupting the translation program. We knew we needed to continue counseling with the same psychologist who, by this time, had

God's Talk

relocated to the SIL International Linguistic Center in Dallas, Texas.

A second compelling reason for our decision was to provide Carrie with a wider choice of friends her own age, language and culture. According to village standards, Carrie by then 13, was of marriageable age. It was unsettling, to say the least, when we heard whiffs of gossip going around that some of the Aztec boys were interested in her as a wife since she could speak the language, grind corn, make tortillas, and wash clothes in the river, all that a good village wife does! In fact she was very reluctant to leave. She said she wanted to continue living among her Aztec friends and ride her horse.

We were still caring for little David and were glad that Genaro's sister and her husband were willing to have him live with them. They did not have children of their own. We had cared for him sixteen months as part of our family. However, it was important that he grow up knowing his biological family, language and culture.

We again closed up the house in Mecayapan, said goodbye to our dear village friends and moved to Texas in August 1974. There was no way to know how long we would be gone this time, but our hope was that, at some point, we could come back and finish the work we had begun.

Work at the International Linguistic Center in Dallas, Texas

On August 8, 1974, we arrived in Duncanville, Texas, a suburb of Dallas. I'll never forget the date--the day we heard that Richard Nixon resigned from the presidency. What a shock that was! A Wycliffe colleague had offered us her furnished house to rent for the school year while she was in Mexico. That was a real answer to our prayer for a place to live in an unfamiliar location. A nice perk was that it was located only a mile from the Center where we would be working.

Carrie registered as an eighth grader and fit right in with her class academically. This was affirmation that the home-school curriculum I had used was adequate. Fifteen other Wycliffe kids her age whose families had recently returned from their overseas assignments provided her with a peer group to pal around with since they all had similar cultural adjustments to make.

It didn't take us long to settle in and feel at home among friendly people. I worked as Center receptionist and secretary at the Linguistic Center for six months. Then in January, I signed up for a three-week course at Baylor University Medical Center in downtown Dallas. It was great to brush up on my stateside nursing skills. After that, Baylor employed me as a staff nurse on the medical-surgical unit.

Marilyn works as a receptionist for the Linguistic Center in Dallas.

Carl was invited to join the Printing Arts Department (PAD) where New Testaments and other literature were processed. On his own time, he continued counseling and worked on two Nahuatl publications: the Gospel of Mark in the Pajapan dialect and the Isthmus Nahuatl Grammar that he was writing in Spanish. Quite a daunting challenge!

We planned to stay at least through the school year to work on the personal problems that had taken us there. As we

Work at the International Linguistic Center in Dallas, Texas

evaluated our progress, however, we were keenly aware that more family stability was important for all of us.

1. We preferred not to disrupt Carrie's high school experience.

2. Carl discovered he worked much better in a highly structured work environment than in a self-directed linguistic and translation program.

3. After a lot of prayer, serious soul-searching and consultations with our director, we made the decision to take extended field trips to the Nahuatl language area so native speakers could help us complete the current language and translation projects.

When our friends would ask, "When are you going back to Mexico?" "What about the Aztecs?" We could only answer that we loved them and God loved them even more. They were His people, not ours. We trusted that in God's timing the Aztec New Testament and other Scriptures would be completed. (As it turned out, we stayed in Dallas over seven years although we also included some extended field trips to Mexico during that time.)

With all this in mind, when a house just two doors down from where we were renting came up for sale, we decided to buy it. We knew we could rent it to other Wycliffe members if we did return to live in Mexico. What a great time the three of us had furnishing and landscaping our very own home--a real haven for us after moving around for 21 years! Decorative shrubbery, a fig tree and a catalpa tree were already there when we bought the house. We planted fruit trees, roses, tulips, daffodils and a small vegetable garden.

God's Talk

We had very little money, but the Lord provided what we needed through a generous loan from Dad Minter. It was extremely exciting.

Field Trip #1

Carl and I took our first field trip to Mecayapan while Carrie spent the summer with good friends. It was great to catch up on all the latest village news about how the believers and churches were doing. Was the water system still functioning? (It was!) Who had gotten married and had new babies? We wanted people to know we had not abandoned them. Nemorio had taken good care of our place, and it looked really nice.

The 3,000 colorful Scripture portions we took along to distribute were received enthusiastically in both the Mecayapan and the Pajapan dialects as well as by believers who came in from the surrounding area. It was encouraging to us that the groups of believers were growing rapidly, and some were using the Nahuatl Scriptures we had left with them. Many were actively reaching out with the Gospel to other villages.

It was gratifying to learn that the Mexican government Department of Education was taking a more active interest in the remote areas by providing bilingual teachers to conduct classes for children and adults on how to improve their crops, put cement floors in their houses, build fire-tables to get their cooking fires off the dirt floors and build fences that would keep animals out of their huts in order to cut down the spread of infectious diseases.

Along with this major development, the government was funding the secondary education for elementary school graduates who spoke both their native language and Spanish to attend high school and teacher training education. Forty-five young people from several Aztec villages were being given this opportunity that year. They were then hired to teach school children back in their own villages in the remote areas. Having their language valued in this way increased the self esteem of our Aztec friends who had been told their language was "gibberish." Before we left, we had a cordial visit with the director who spearheaded this program in our area. We came away optimistic that positive changes are happening.

On our return to Dallas, Carl continued his work in the Publications Department at ILC. This included typesetting several New Testaments. Linguistic and anthropology books were in the pipeline, too. The six staff members were swamped. Typists worked steadily on New Testament manuscripts sent in by translators from countries around the world. Seven New Testaments were in process at that time.

Carl works on typesetting a New Testament in the Printing Arts Department at the Linguistic Center in Dallas.

God's Talk

Each of these languages had special requirements for typesetting, and each translator had their preferences for formatting. Having been a translator himself, Carl could appreciate "fussy" clients! With his excellent computer skills and a tendency to perfectionism, he was a great asset in this type of work. He also oriented new personnel on their way to the field and learned to troubleshoot typesetting problems for the field installations.

By this time Carl and I were satisfied that we were at the right place so we requested to be "home assigned" indefinitely at the International Linguistic Center. Home assigned members were not on a salary but were faith-based, as all Wycliffe members were, regardless of their responsibilities or assignments. They trust the Lord to provide through faithful financial and prayer partners. Home assigned support personnel were considered to be as important to the Bible Translation mission as foreign assigned members. But some who supported us in Mexico chose to decrease their giving or drop it altogether when they learned we had a home assignment. Even though we were disappointed, we were so grateful that most of our financial partners chose to hang in there with us, and some even increased their support.

Carl reflects on attachment to village house:

> *Being home assigned means that at some point we need to make a decision about what to do with our house and its contents in Mecayapan. I consulted with my supervisor who said he thinks that it is wise to go ahead and sell our village house in Mexico. I am having real problems with that when it comes right down to it. Today I realized that I am more attached to our house--"our place"--than to the people. I want to hold on to it. I realized this was part of the dissatisfaction, irritation and*

Work at the International Linguistic Center in Dallas, Texas

frustration I often felt with people. There is so much sentiment attached to all the things I made for Marilyn and Carrie--the time and effort that I spent to make my family comfortable, to build a 'nest'.

In 1977 our busy family was happily involved in the local Presbyterian Church. Carl directed the choir, Carrie was active in the youth group, and I was elected to the board of elders. Carrie, as an eleventh grader, was a teacher's assistant in Biology and active in drama club and a Bible Study for Wycliffe Kids. She also worked part-time, first at Braum's ice cream store and then at KFC. She was invited to sing and play her guitar on various occasions.

I terminated my work at Baylor and worked part-time in the Wycliffe Regional Office making telephone calls and writing letters, arranging for Wycliffe members to speak and/or show films on requests from churches, missions conferences, college chapels, etc. Twice a week I braved heavy Dallas traffic to drive 90 miles round trip to Denton for graduate classes at Texas Woman's University.

Sunday evenings we met together with the Wycliffe family and were inspired by the reports given by our Wycliffe colleagues who came through the Linguistic Center on their way to or from their fields of service. For example:

- The Jicaque tribe in Honduras had been extremely opposed to the Gospel. Translators worked 17 years on Scripture before the Jicaque chief, along with a dozen others in the tribe, publicly accepted the Lord.
- One translation team reported that for several months the camera-ready Kamano-Kafe New Testament was thought to be lost somewhere between Papua New

Guinea and Hong Kong where it was to be printed. It was uncanny how snags could hold up work on the Scriptures. PNG staff prepared to have it re-typeset until, several weeks later, the manuscript surprisingly turned up at the Hong Kong Bible Society. A staff member had carefully put it on a shelf without telling anyone it had arrived! The printing promptly moved forward and was soon into the hearts of the Kamano-Kafe people. Another language that will be heard around the throne in Heaven!

Clinic Services

In the spring of 1978, the Center administration became more keenly aware of the critical need for medical services for members with serious physical and emotional health problems as they transitioned to and from their assignments. Their needs were often not addressed due to transient schedules, high costs of office visits, medicine, diagnostic tests and counseling.

Wycliffe members who were medical professionals gathered for a three-day conference at the Center to discuss how to formally initiate a department of Member Health Services and work through the legal ramifications. A consensus was reached to set up a clinic. They asked if I would be willing to coordinate this new start-up service. With some trepidation, I accepted the position as Director of Clinical services. I then resigned my job at the Wycliffe Regional Office.

Six months earlier a Wycliffe nurse had offered to consult informally with members about their health needs. She had been given permission to use the tiny janitor's closet at the end of the student dormitory. After cleaning it thoroughly, she furnished it with a donated ancient exam table, a small table with two wobbly chairs for consultations, a few rudimentary supplies and donated medicine samples kept on two rickety shelves. It was a primitive, crowded space, to be sure, but a place where members could talk confidentially. This was what I had to work with as I started daily clinic services.

Two local physicians in private practice graciously volunteered their services three half-days a week to do physical exams, vaccinations, lab work and consultations. But we needed a doctor who was familiar with tropical diseases to treat members returning from assignments in countries where parasites and other debilitating diseases abound.

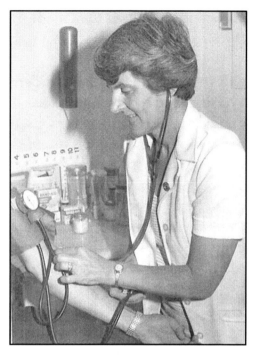

Marilyn was in charge of the clinic at the Linguistic Center in Dallas.

This new adventure was like pioneering. I winged it as I went along since I had no written job description to go by. Volunteer nurses helped me staff the clinic on a rotating basis. After a few months in the cramped cleaning closet, I was allowed to expand the clinic space and relieve the congestion by using the dormitory room next door.

A year later it was a great relief when Dr. Ralph Eichenberger, Wycliffe member from the Peru branch, agreed to come on a full-time basis. He was well versed in tropical diseases. His wife Beth, a registered lab technician, set up the clinic laboratory. Together they made a winning combination for the Health Services.

Our clients were linguistic students, new applicants to Wycliffe, and a large international staff. Wycliffe colleagues on furlough for medical reasons, advanced study programs or counseling made good use of the clinic, too. New members preparing for their overseas assignments were given thorough medical exams, extensive lab work, psychological screening, vaccinations, and teaching with emphasis on health management and prevention of illness in primitive conditions. The total number of people served in our first six months was over 500!

The Center administrator worked with me on floor plans for a permanent, free-standing clinic building that would accommodate medical, dental and mental health services, with at least one full-time Wycliffe doctor, a dentist and three counselors. It wasn't until 1983 that this dream came to fruition and is now being used to maximum capacity. It's delightful to visit the clinic and see how our dream came true! Thank you, Lord.

Work at the International Linguistic Center in Dallas, Texas

Field Trip #2

To show just how tedious daily language work can be in laying the groundwork for good Scripture translation, we include notes from Carl's journal.

May 2 - July 9, 1978. Trip to Mecayapan and Pajapan to Work on the Nahuatl Grammar.

> --- *A welcome piece of news! The telegram from Gonzalo today says he wants to work with me on the Nahuatl grammar. He is in his twenties, is bilingual in Spanish and Nahuatl and a very capable person to work on this project. He is one of the few Mecayapan young people who has completed secondary school. He contributed to the dictionary, was oriented in linguistics and has been trained to make primers for literacy classes.*
>
> --- *With nervous trepidation I flew American Airlines from Dallas to Mexico City carrying my precious cargo--all our linguistic data and the irreplaceable dictionary files. Had a good flight. Waited an hour to get a ticket for the midnight bus to Acayucan. It's vacation time so the terminal was crowded.*
>
> --- *Arrived in Mecayapan at 2:00 p.m. ready to get to work. Gonzalo wants to volunteer his time <u>without pay</u>. What a gift! The frogs and dry-season locusts are singing; loudspeaker blaring across town. Tomorrow I plan to go to Pajapan to check on how the brethren are doing there.*
>
> --- *It took me about five hours to get to Pajapan where I met with Demetrio, one of the brethren there. He told me of a split in their church group when Pedro claimed the building belonged to him because it was on his land. Nicolas and most of the congregation left Salem Church and joined up with Prince*

God's Talk

of Peace church. I hope they can resolve it peacefully. A big, new church building is being built--30 x 75 feet--just a shell so far. They use it with dirt floor, open doorways and windows.

Demetrio invited me for supper at his house. Then Erasto and Roman came home from their fields near nightfall. They inquired about the translation of the Gospel of Mark we had done together last year in the Pajapan dialect. They were delighted with the manuscript samples I brought with me. Nicolas, Roman, Gerardo and I went through the manuscript verse by verse. We corrected about 40 verses that needed work. We finished at 1:00 a.m. Nicolas got sleepy and conked out before midnight but the other two did real well.

--- Had chacalin (shrimp), mamey fruit and some delicious Pajapan pan dulce (sweet bread) for breakfast.

(Later, back in Mecayapan) Haven't seen Gonzalo yet today. Elodia is doing my laundry. Bless her heart, she came around very quickly to get my tzotzol (dirty clothes). Had dinner with Professor Enrique and his wife. Met the director of the Cultural Mission. They invited me to have cena (evening meal) with them later this evening. Visited with Epifaneo and little David. He's nearly five years old now. He came right up and stayed close to me. Then when we were about to leave, Epi showed him how to say goodbye with a big hug and kiss for itajhuehuej (his "old grandfather"). He warmed my heart!

I decided to store our stuff in the rat-proof closet so someone can rent our house temporarily. Rental of the house would justify keeping it for now. If another translation team takes our place and wants to use it, they will at least have that option. Gonzalo said a phone is to be installed very shortly in Mecaya-

Work at the International Linguistic Center in Dallas, Texas

pan--imagine that! Pajapan and Tatahuicapan already have the type of phone that uses microwaves from a tower.

--- G[onzalo] and I took the bus to Mexico City and arrived at the Ixmiquilpan workshop center about noon after an all-night ride. I arranged for someone to bring my luggage that I left in the city. Otherwise, I'll run out of clothes real fast. It's really quiet here, no other language helpers here at present, so Gonzalo may feel like a lone sheep. He's rather timid so I don't want to push him into contact with too many people at once. Like tonight, he chose not to go to the Spanish sing-a-long. I want to look carefully at the Otomi grammar as well as some others to get an idea of how to proceed on mine. Doris Bartholomew said she's available to consult with us until she leaves for her teaching assignment in June.

--- Today was a busy day consulting, reading, and typing. Doris has lots of helpful suggestions. It's easier to write in Spanish again since getting back into the language. Gonzalo and I went to the amazing Monday morning country market and bought fresh fruits and vegetables. I fixed our meals today but tomorrow we're invited out for dinner. Mary Jane Dedrick gave me her recipe for quick-cook beans using the pressure cooker so I'll refry some for breakfast and supper tomorrow.

I was outside getting some fresh air when Jane Nellis brought over a loaf of fresh home-made bread. We had some for supper along with the beans. It was delicious. Amy Bauernschmidt brought my luggage from the city, so I'm in good shape now.

I brought both of our typewriters and G[onzalo] does a neat typing job so he is typing the Nahuatl word lists and corrects details of my Spanish translation. I'm very glad for his willingness to do that. He likes my Olympia typewriter so well that he wants to buy it. I haven't yet found a good way to spark his *creative imagination for categorizing or describing the grammatical things.*

--- Since his father has a gas stove, Gonzalo would like to know how to bake bread so Jane Nellis' maid came over this morning and showed us how to do it. The bread turned out really good -- like **bolillos franceses** *(french rolls) made with water and very little shortening.*

--- I feel good about the work we did today. Things are beginning to come together. Doris thinks we should include the Pajapan word list that Marilyn copied in pencil. It should be an asset to the grammar.

This place is sure isolated as far as news is concerned. No radio or daily newspaper. I haven't the faintest idea what's happening in the world. Someone brought some English newspapers from the city several days old.

--- Long day today. The manuscript is getting thicker. So is my head, I think. Gonzalo is checking and filling in the word list. Details! I've kept free of depressed, gloomy feelings for the most part. Gonzalo is a steady, adaptable person, more talkative now that he is catching on to what we're trying to accomplish. At first he was so reserved and hesitant to talk.

Spent some time this evening looking through a couple of the grammars in other Nahuatl dialects but they don't have the same usage as our **cuayoj** *(forest) and* **ocoyoj** *(pine grove). So I'll just have to set it forth as it is used and say how different it is from the -yoj in soquiyoj and tajyoj. Oh, I could write a book about it. Say, that's what I'm doing!* **Ma taj de veras!** *(Hey, that's right!)*

Work at the International Linguistic Center in Dallas, Texas

If an apartment is still available when the workshop ends, we may stay here longer. It's cheaper than at headquarters in the City. But there we have meals prepared, dishes washed for us and more activities to break the monotony. Gonzalo wants to bake bread again. I'll do the laundry too, no clean underwear. Batching it is for the birds. I had some intestinal bug yesterday. Didn't get anything done in the afternoon. Feel better this morning. Hunger pangs now, guess that's a good sign.

--- Started reading "Future Shock" last evening. We're definitely out of step with modern society by keeping our old car for 12 years. This author's presentation of the great sweep of human history doesn't even pay lip service to Jesus Christ in any of the parts I've read. Won't he be in for a shock when he finds out who's been in charge all this time?

--- Well, now I've progressed from describing Nahuatl nouns to describing Nahuatl adjectives . Another two to three days and I'll describe the Nahuatl adverbs. I have tentatively described some of them, but they need to be reorganized. Then it's on to conjunctions, relative pronouns and more verbs. I have finished the introduction in Spanish.

--- I have returned to headquarters with Gonzalo who is staying in the men's dorm with other language helpers. Found a satisfactory place for us to work together. Visited with Jim and Juanita Watters. He is teaching linguistics courses to Mexican young people here. One of Gonzalo's instructors from the school in Acayucan is here taking the linguistics course. G[onzalo] is pleased someone is here that he knows personally. This man, Alonzo Lopez Mar, is a consultant for primers. He has funds for publications and is much interested in this type

of material. We trust that more meaningful contacts can be made later.

--- Gonzalo is impressed with the complexity of the Aztec language. Today he remarked that native stories translated into Spanish just don't come out the same. They sound better in Nahuatl! He read the Bible parables we had translated about the lost coin, sheep, etc. and said that they are bonito (beautiful). We've been reading in Romans for our daily devotional times but he hasn't yet commented about anything in that.

--- Working on describing adverbials. They are so complex and interesting to me. We have to describe many things that work so differently from Spanish. Progress slow today. I've worked until my head is numb! Doris will need to take a last look before the final touches are added. Artemisa checked some of the verbs yesterday and made a few minor corrections in the Spanish. It is now ready to present to the school coordinator in Acayucan.

--- Went with Gonzalo to a Spanish speaking church this morning. He enjoyed it too. The sound system was good. Visited the Zocalo and went up the Latin American Tower. Only 10 pesos. Always an impressive sight. Metro still costs only one peso. We both ate dinner with Jim and Juanita. Talked Spanish through most of the meal. Jim converses well in Spanish considering the short time he has studied it.

--- Almost a month has passed since I began work on this project. Have gotten rather bogged down recently. Want to evaluate where we are--it is coming out rougher than I would like. Hard to achieve a balance. It's coming along, slow but sure--final results do add up to something.

Work at the International Linguistic Center in Dallas, Texas

I'm thankful we are both keeping well. Except for that first day or two at Ixmi I've felt fine--eating chiles and all. The meal schedule here at Tlalpan is much to my liking, and I enjoy the Mexican touches. When some rather nondescript, mediocre American-style food is served I wish for more Mexican food!

--- Wednesday morning, and it's a beautiful sunny morning. I opened the door to let some of it in. It's been quite chilly part of the time here in the city. Real good for working. My poor old tweedy jacket is getting a work-out every day. I discovered a big moth hole under one lapel. Guess it's ready to be replaced.

Today I described more difficult adverbial constructions. Lots of loose ends to pick up before I leave July 10. Visited with Alonzo Lopez Mar, the fellow from Acayucan who's taking the linguistics course.. He is pretty high up in Mexican bilingual education and has a very insightful approach to the indigenous person's low self-image. He is an Aztec from the Huasteca area and had some good suggestions for Gonzalo's primer project.

--- Spent all day checking the spelling of the Nahuatl vocabulary list. Arranged subentries and checked for accuracy. My purpose was to extrapolate all the verbs to give myself a set of 3 x 5 slips to finalize the verb classes and the rules that go with them. But I needed to be sure of vowel length, etc. so decided to get that taken care of for the whole word list.

I am disappointed that Gonzalo hasn't yet grasped the spelling in Nahuatl. For awhile I panicked when I saw how much work the vocabulary needs just to get the Nahuatl side in shape. Decided that is second in priority and will do what I can after the rest of the job is done. Vocabulary is just a "teaser" until the real dictionary comes out, anyway. I look forward to getting back to the grammar again tomorrow after a day's respite. Artemisa checked over everything that I've done so far--made

God's Talk

notes on where to improve my Spanish. She's very thorough. Some pages need to be retyped before I show it to the director in Acayucan.

--- I accepted Karen Bronson's invitation to have supper with them and then go to a concert. It's in a new concert hall near the National University. The Orquesta del Estado de Mexico (the Orchestra of the State of Mexico) did a thrilling rendition of Beethoven's 9th Symphony with a tremendous chorus and soloists. Bronson's friend plays in the orchestra and had complimentary tickets for us.

For devotional time, it's encouraging to see Gonzalo eagerly pick up Romans for our daily Bible reading. We read a section first in Spanish, then in Nahuatl. He said, "It comes out clearer in Nahuatl!" So far he hasn't asked any questions or made comments about it. I can only trust the exposure will bear fruit in his life.

--- We attended a lecture in Spanish on the History of Linguistics in Mexico. Gonzalo said ,"I see that linguistics is very important." The irregular verbs are done now. I want to display a model of each type in all tenses, including all irregular tenses. Will consult with Artemisa this afternoon.

--- Gonzalo was impressed with the sermon at the church we attended this morning. He asked if I could get him some Bibles in Spanish to take back to Mecayapan. Will stop and get those on the way when I take him to the bus station this evening. He wants to attend the next linguistics course in Oaxaca next month.

--- I'd like to go home this month (June) but I think I'll stick to it here while things are still fresh on my mind and while

Work at the International Linguistic Center in Dallas, Texas

Artemisa is here to help check my Spanish. (Spanish is her first language.)

Ramona Millar is driving to Dallas July 8th and asked if I would travel with her. I'd prefer to fly, but I'm inclined to say I'll travel with her. It's not an easy decision to make. I have enough money left over to fly since Gonzalo didn't want any pay.

--- Thurs. morning. Just had coffee with my roommate, Rick, who is here studying Mexican cuisine for a TV show he produces. He is nearly through his doctorate in linguistics at Michigan State University. His wife suddenly left him last year and wouldn't consider working things out, so he has had a pretty rough year. They were married four and a half years. It's hard to hear about such break-ups.

Last night in the dining room, where I was working on the write-up of long vowels, I cornered Saul, our Mexican colleague who edits grammars for good Spanish, to ask him to review the pages I had just finished. Both little and big things needed improvement. It takes a native speaker to edit a manuscript so it results in excellent Spanish. Really sounded good when he got done with it!

--- The strains of the song "Las Mañanitas" are coming in through the open window. Today I'll put the final touches on the manuscript then will make copies for Gonzalo and the linguistics coordinator. I get lots of remarks about the long hours I spend working at the table in the dining room.

--- Visited for two hours in the library with our friend Thelma, who is a professor in linguistics at the University of Mexico.

God's Talk

She likes my manuscript and is fascinated with the presentation. She xeroxed the whole 200 pages for herself yesterday.

--- I just finished eating two bowls of hot celery soup with whole wheat bread. Very satisfying. Made a drink from hot tap water, a spoonful of honey and a few grains of instant Nescafe coffee. Tasted so good. My room is near the boilers, so tap water is very hot. Tomorrow, July 9, I return to Dallas. I'm ready to be home again!

After Carl returned, the three of us spent two pleasant weeks of vacation relaxing in the beautiful Colorado Rocky Mountains. It was awesome driving down through the Big Thompson River Canyon where two years before the big flood had killed so many people and destroyed businesses. That year Mom and Dad Minter worked with Mennonite Disaster Services to help the Sylvan Guest Ranch Bed and Breakfast dig out of the deep, oozy mud. Out of curiosity, we stopped there to see what it looked like and couldn't tell it had been covered with mud ten inches deep! The owners invited us to a delicious barbecue supper along the river. They couldn't get done expressing appreciation for the way the clean-up crew helped them recover their business.

Lots of clinic work was waiting for me when I returned from vacation. A family came from Africa with severe symptoms of filariasis, a parasitic infection that abounds in that part of the world but is rarely seen in the U.S. Dr. Eichenberger thoroughly researched what was needed for proper diagnosis, tests and treatment. They recovered satisfactorily. A family from Indonesia had relapses of malaria. A translator from Peru returned with leishmaniasis, a painful, tissue-destroying tropical ulcer. Medicine was available only through the Communicable Disease Center in Atlanta. After making a phone call, the medicine was on its way!

Field Trip #3 - December 1977

This time we needed God's guidance about whether to sell our house in the village, or keep it for another team to use. The three of us made another trip to Mecayapan. Our main reason this time was two-fold: to finalize some technical language research data and decide whether to sell our village house and belongings.

Marilyn give the details of the trip:

> We had a smooth border crossing at Brownsville and an overnight stop at Ciudad Victoria at Hotel Palacio. The ferry at Tampico had two lines of vehicles waiting to cross. We waited two and a half hours to cross on the ferry. In the meantime, our car sat in a big puddle of muddy water so it got splashed mightily when a truck tried to pass. We watched drivers squeeze through tight spots and wade through the muddy water. We watched an angry confrontation between a truck driver and a taxi driver at a narrow spot. The taxi driver conceded by backing down the street again. A bus came barreling past us just as Carrie opened the window and again we got splashed with icky brown water!
>
> Overnight at Hotel Los Mangos in Tuxpan where we were offered a half-warmed-over supper at the hotel's buffet. Read stories aloud in Nahuatl to brush up on the language. Visited the Tajin ruins; saw the **voladores** (Totonac pole dancers) *fly* around the pole. Picnicked along the beach. Followed the coast-

God's Talk

line, waded in the beautiful, clear blue ocean. Bought a bunch of tangerines and two fresh pineapples on the way to Alvarado.

The next night we stayed at Hotel Castellanos at Veracruz, a new six-story round building with our room on the fifth floor, a gorgeous view to the hills and a beautiful pastoral scene with pretty red-tiled roofs beneath us. It sported plush wall to wall carpeting, an elevator, hand-painted decorations on the wash bowls and faucet knobs. We watched a Christmas procession go by the sidewalk cafe where we ate a late supper.

On arrival in our market town of Acayucan, the Casa Iglesias grocery store was about to close for the afternoon siesta so we quickly stocked up with groceries and wended our way to Mecayapan.

The rats and cockroaches had had a hey-day in our house for the three years while we were gone. There was no serious damage, though. We cleaned it up as best we could and enjoyed our time there. The electricity went off the day after we arrived and didn't come on again till the day we left. We were back to using kerosene lamps. So what else is new?

Our Aztec friends gave us a warm welcome as always and were eager to share with us their joys and sorrows, victories and disappointments. Oh, yes, and FOOD. We loved those thick, warm, tender corn tortillas with delicious chicken soup and black beans. It doesn't get any better than that. By the time we left we had accumulated 40 pounds of black beans that people gave us to bring home.

John and Royce Lind came down the mountain from their village to celebrate Christmas Eve with us around our fireplace and stayed overnight at our house. It was a very special time with dear friends. For Christmas Day dinner all of us hiked back up the trail to their place in Ocotal Chico. More good food and a visit in the afternoon, just like old times.

We were delighted and encouraged to see signs of spiritual, economic and educational progress among the Aztec people. There were five growing congregations. Luke and his group now read the Scriptures in Nahuatl. In two groups, the colorful banners we made long ago with Nahuatl verses were still hanging in each chapel and still looked nice. They decorate them with lots of color.

Our next door neighbor, Antonio, had accepted the Lord after his son died several months before. His wife hadn't "entered in" yet. More young people were bilingual teachers or vocational students. Victor, one of our neighbor boys then 19, was home on vacation from his new teaching job. He thanked Carl for patiently teaching him to type on our old battered typewriter four years earlier and said it helped him a lot in his teaching job. Many young people came around to our reading table. They proudly used their mother tongue much more in conversation, due to the government fostering preservation of the language and the literature we've published.

We decided not to sell the house yet, but did sell some equipment. The proceeds just about paid for the trip. Carrie sold her two horses. People had money from having sold their coffee and black bean crops.

God's Talk

Observations on this trip:

- People liked the Spanish Bibles we brought so we wanted to connect with a source in Mexico City; that way one or more of the storekeepers there could keep a supply.
- A lady was teaching embroidery, knitting and crocheting to the girls.
- Gonzalo's father, "Fred," was attending one of the groups of believers in the village. He was very sincere and emphasized our unity in Christ.
- The boys who came around seemed more well-behaved and interested in reading both in Nahuatl and in Spanish.
- More girls were able to read.
- Most of the girls who were Carrie's age had gone on to secondary school and vocational training. They were waiting longer to marry.

Observations about people in the village:

- **Genaro** had finished a three-year stint in the army and was in school. He bought some of our books and mentioned how the book of Romans was a big help to him. He was also interested in linguistics. His second marriage hadn't worked out, and he had a struggle with alcoholism but did express a real desire to be in fellowship with the Lord in his life. His son David, who lived with us after his mother died, still remembered us!
- **Zacarias** still kept a neat store. He was interested in the grammar and was very congenial.
- **Gonzalo** was taking training at Acayucan and was interested in the grammar that we had worked on.
- **Sabina** (one of Carrie's girlfriends) was the main cook at the boarding school kitchen there. She had had a concrete

block house built for herself and a shiny new stove delivered.
- **Elodia** brought us *tatiquetzal* (crisp tortillas) and 10 pesos to buy eggs because she couldn't find any at their rancho. That was the first time anyone had given us money to buy a local product! Her family looked cleaner this time.
- **Esteban** bought our ice cream freezer for 80 pesos.
- **Sylvia's sisters,** Marcela, Sarita and Susanna came to visit. Sarita had a deep voice and rapid speech. She hadn't gone to school but was working as a maid in the Health Center. Marcela went to school and would finish sixth grade that year. Susanna was still home.

December 31, 1977 - New Year's Eve

We arrived home again after a harrowing experience at the Mexico/US border at Laredo where a political rally was causing traffic to back up for miles in the hot sun. It was good to cross into the good old USA.

Significant events in 1979:

Carrie celebrated the magical passage into adulthood on her 18th birthday March 6. She played the role of "Maria" to a packed audience in her high school play, The Sound of Music. The entire cast did a fantastic job!

On our 25th wedding anniversary we celebrated at Pepe's Mexican Restaurant in North Dallas by inviting another couple to ride with us in the snazzy Ford Thunderbird that Carl rented as a complete surprise for me.

We participated in the community Chorale that performed excerpts of Mendelssohn's oratorio Elijah along with the

God's Talk

Dallas Symphony Orchestra under the direction of Eric Kunzel. Carl took a computer course at Mountain View College, and I took another graduate course in psychology and counseling at Texas Woman's University.

One of our friends helped us finalize a real estate deal at the Dallas/Duncanville city line--two and a half country acres with the charming name of Crystal Lake Apartments, but no lake! Clustered along the long driveway east of the house were ten small, rustic rental cottages that the owners themselves, a retired couple, had built years before. Being a landlord and keeping tenants happy turned out to be more than we bargained for. As the rental cottages were vacated we did a modest upgrade on them. This was a whole new stretching experience for us.

We moved into the large ranch-style three-bedroom brick house with two-car garage. The former owners were heavy chain smokers, so the whole house reeked with stale smoke. Walls and woodwork were coated with sticky residue from many years of cigarette smoke. It took lots of hard work to make the house livable. Friends from church helped us scour walls, woodwork, wash drapes and shampoo the carpet. To our delight, a huge fenced-in vegetable garden was already planted. A workshop, fruit trees and large grassy areas completed the bucolic country scene. That much grass-mowing was a major undertaking. It was fun, though, to host informal groups of our friends for picnics on our spacious lawn.

That summer Carrie graduated from High School, bought herself a Volkswagen, had braces put on her teeth, worked as teller at a local bank and explored college options for the fall.

I continued my job at the Center Clinic and discovered that sometimes an empathetic listening ear helped as much as medicine. We had a wonderful, efficient network of doctors whose hearts were for missions, and they understood the unique circumstances missionaries live in.

Carl worked faithfully with teams who came through to submit their New Testament manuscripts for processing. Each one was precious! Another big project he helped develop was the format for an Auxiliary Translation Commentary. It was described as an "enhanced amplified version." Selected notes on each verse were edited by Wycliffe's experts in the Translation Department. This was a real boost to the translation teams on the field.

Carrie registered at Central College in McPherson, Kansas, a Free Methodist Church college. We drove her there along with her much-loved guitar "Herbie," plus all the other things a teenager seemed to need. The house was so empty without Carrie to liven it up. We missed her as she left the nest. It was just the two of us again.

As people came to the clinic with personal problems, I began to realize just how closely linked physical, emotional and spiritual struggles were. I felt the need for more training in counseling, so I registered for a degree program in psychology at nearby Dallas Baptist University. A generous scholarship from Mary Crowley, the founder of Home Interiors

God's Talk

Decorations and generous benefactor of missions, covered all my expenses. Bless her!

It has been suggested that older adults often make the best students. It was a great day of rejoicing when, at age 50, I graduated magna cum laude with a BS degree in psychology and counseling.

Field Trip # 4 - November 1979

Carl spent another six-week stint with Gonzalo in Mexico to work on the manuscript that described in great detail the Grammar of the Nahuatl language. I was fearful for their safety because of the political turmoil in Mexico and could only trust God for Carl's safe return.

Significant events were taking place in the Mexico Branch which would affect all of the filed teams and our SIL colleagues and. A strong nationalistic movement was growing, and some officials opposed the presence of SIL members in the ethnic communities.

At the end of 1979, the branch director was officially notified that the one-year visas held by many of our members would not be renewed at the time of their expiration. This caused much confusion and disruption as they and their families had to leave and establish themselves in their home country. Over two-thirds of the members left Mexico through the next year. It was traumatic for the whole branch and left a minimum staff of members with permanent visas to carry on operations at the centers. Branch leaders did what they could to establish support for those who were leaving and to put into place practices that would enable the work to continue. They also sought to find Mexican officials and friends in responsible positions who could advise why these changes had taken place and to find out if there were possibilities for modification of the new policies. But these efforts were unsuccessful even though some officials in important positions did what they could to help. Another aspect of the turmoil was the abundance of negative media coverage directed at SIL (ILV).

A result of this turmoil was that a new center of operation was developed in Arizona where work continued. Indigenous co-workers were able to spend periods of time there with the SIL people who had been working in their village areas and continue with translation, literacy and linguistic projects. By the beginning of 1988, political winds were changing again, and visas began to be available to SIL members in small numbers. Little by little teams returned to Mexico, and fortunately, at this time the people who need visas have been able to get them, and to continue their work in Mexico.

Field Trip #5 - February 1980

Carl and I drove to Mecayapan for the main purpose of closing out our work and selling the adobe house that we had lived in with all its simplicity and rusticity. Antonio, our next door neighbor, told us he wanted to buy it. He sold two of his cattle and paid us $18,000 pesos. We shared part of the proceeds with Howard and Joan Law since they had built the house 20 years earlier.

We had a public sale of all our personal property in the house. This in itself was an emotionally wrenching experience for both of us. It was equally hard for us to give up the

God's Talk

idea that we couldn't finish the New Testament as we had hoped.

I took the midnight bus from Acayucan to Mexico City, boarded a plane to Dallas and continued my study program while Carl stayed in the village for another three weeks to finalize the myriad of details on the Grammar with Gonzalo and turn in the manuscript for publication. Their diligent work paid off brilliantly. It was soon ready for publication. Five hundred copies were printed and a second printing was needed later due to demand by government officials and teachers in the Aztec area schools.

Carl writes of mixed feelings:

> *I had mixed feelings about selling off our stuff--a sense of release from the weight of the enormous responsibility I had been carrying mixed with sadness to be leaving permanently.*

> *The beautiful part, though, about visiting the field where one has invested years of effort is to see people continue to serve the Lord. Chencho is one of those people. He first trusted Christ through the witness of Howard and Joan Law. Later he worked with both Marilyn and me on Scripture translation. He circulated the Gospel Recordings of the translated Scriptures from one Aztec village and thatched-roof hut to another, and the response to them was heartening. The Scriptures that we translated together have touched many hearts.*

> *Chencho credits us with saving his life. When we returned from a workshop one year, we found him terribly wasted away from tuberculosis. He would surely have died, as many others here have if we hadn't taken him to the public health clinic 40 miles away for the treatment he needed. We praised the Lord*

that we could have a part in saving his life. He has led more people to faith in Christ than anyone else we know in this language area. He has nurtured the growing groups of believers scattered through the surrounding countryside. Seeing him healthy again made our trip worthwhile.

One thing I remember with special warmth is that Chencho would take time to pray with us. He would simply wish us God's blessing and protection when we were about to leave the village for the "vast unknown" (to him) of Mexico City or even the vaster unknown of Los Estados Unidos (The United States). His sincere concern for us was always touching.

Genaro's story is a very sad one. Soon after Marilyn's departure, I was alone when he and Adrian, another young Aztec man, appeared at my door one evening shortly before nightfall, obviously having been drinking. I had just wrapped up the sale of our village house for the price of two cows and was sitting down to eat a bowl of beans by myself. I had been told earlier that Genaro and Adrian were gaining a reputation for meanness when they were drunk. When they asked if they could come in, it didn't seem to me they were that drunk. I was wrong. They had not come merely to chat.

Genaro soon made it clear to me that he intended to make sure I did not leave the village without giving him some tangible "remembrance of our long association." Yes, it had been a long association. From the earliest days of our work in Mecayapan, at age 15, he had helped us learn the language. As time went by he professed faith in Christ.

We had done a lot for Genaro. We had sponsored and supported him through school. He had seemed so sincere about his faith, teaching and helping his people. We helped him through the death of his young wife and took care of his little boy David for

God's Talk

16 months afterwards till he could get back on his feet emotionally. At other times, though, he spoke with disdain of his home town and expressed a wish to leave it behind. Perhaps it was this desire to escape that led to his increased love affair with alcohol. He couldn't seem to get hold of his life, and our association pretty much ended there.

Now there he was that evening, bitter, threatening, emboldened by drink and by recent contact with Marxist ideology beamed over the radio from Cuba, alleging that I and my colleagues "had earned academic degrees and gotten rich at the expense of lowly informants like himself who gave us the secrets of their language in exchange for peon's wages and insipid American food." He mistakenly believed the Bible teaches the poor to be submissive so that the rich can take advantage of them! The noise of their diatribe attracted the attention of neighbors who called for the authorities to come. Before any actual violence was done, a small group of men came to the house and persuaded my two young visitors to leave quietly, but not before Genaro had reached into my shirt pocket and grabbed my little calculator and pen. We hurt for Genaro!

The above incident with Genaro could have turned out so much differently had our friends not intervened. People there must have assumed that Carl would be carrying a lot of money from the sale of the house and its contents. So again, it was providential that no one accosted him along the road as he left Mecayapan by himself the next day. We like to think it was out of respect and the legacy of the Scriptures we left with them.

Wedding of our Daughter

Our daughter Carrie married Mark Christopher on May 30, 1980. The day dawned bright and beautiful--a perfect day for a wedding. It was a meaningful ceremony in the Free Methodist Church with nearly 200 friends and family present.

As if a wedding wasn't stressful enough for me, five days later I underwent major surgery complicated by adhesions from previous surgery. I was under anesthesia five hours due to complications. It took several weeks to recuperate. Friends brought meals in, helped with household tasks and assured us of their prayers.

Moving On

During a week of blistering August days, we were invited to be "missionaries in residence" at a Christian Youth Camp near Watonga, Oklahoma. I still wasn't quite up to par from my recent surgery, but I made it through the week. We shared what's involved in Bible Translation with sixty alert young people eager to hear about missions.

Back in full swing by the fall of 1980, our clinic staff was given permission to move from the "broom closet" in the dormitory to a large mobile unit up on the hill. This gave us much more space to treat patients and do lab work. I continued to pursue studies in psychology and counseling in order to do a better job of meeting people's needs wholistically--body, mind, soul and spirit. Colleagues and co-workers frequently shared with me how Health Services had met a real need for them.

God's Talk

More than 800 staff, students, administrative personnel, retirees, members in training, missionaries on furlough, and their children now lived and worked on or around the campus of the International Linguistic Center. It was like a small city! The workload at the Health Center increased significantly as our medical staff consulted with 15-25 people a day about their health needs.

In January 1981, much prayer went up for Chester "Chet" Bitterman, a Wycliffe translator in Colombia who was taken hostage by terrorists and later was killed. Chet and his wife Brenda had been students at the Linguistic Center a few years before, so it was a personal tragedy for the whole Wycliffe family. His capture, death and the continued terrorist threats to other teams all served to remind us of the harsh reality that we were in a life and death struggle to spread the Gospel. Capture and death were no longer a vague unspoken fear but was right out where the issue had to be faced: "Yes, I may die for my decision to share God's Word."

Carl filled a key position in the Publications Department, getting the translation for the Shapra/Candoshi group of Peru ready to publish. Sheila Tuggy, one of the translators, wrote, "The Shapra and Candoshi Christians are following the Lord so completely. The head-hunters who have resisted the Word all these years are now asking if someone will teach them. Hatred has turned to love through the translated Word. It is great to see God work in people's lives." What a privilege it was to help it happen!

This was the language spoken by Tariri, the Shapra chief and former head-hunter whose conversion to Christ was depicted in the large mural at the 1964 New York World's Fair while we were there on staff. Chief Tariri himself came to New York and was at the Fair for a short while. At that time

Work at the International Linguistic Center in Dallas, Texas

only limited portions were in his heart language. Now his people had the whole New Testament.

Working as the computer process analyst at the Printing Arts Department, Carl carried heavy responsibilities. Along with other duties, he developed a computer-based hyphenation algorithm (a sequence of steps) for the New Testament manuscripts that were brought in by translators for processing. He told me that he considered it to be fun as he looked for patterns in each language and then programmed the computer accordingly! He explained it this way.

Each translator gave him specific instructions for the rules of how his/her particular language must be hyphenated at the end of lines so that it made sense to the reader. Given all this information, Carl then figured out how to program the computer to correctly hyphenate words automatically throughout the printing process. There were usually a few exceptions to the rules that had to be figured in as well.

The contribution Carl made proved to be a big boost to the whole process. We were informed later that this hyphenation routine was still being used for New Testament manuscripts thirty years later!

Maintaining the large property where we lived added a mixture of stress and pleasure. The country setting was peaceful. However, those two stressful jobs exacerbated the troubling personal inner struggles that Carl had been fighting for several years and increased the problems that had plagued our marriage. He ended up going into a specialized intensive treatment program with a Christian psychotherapist. These months were filled with anxiety for me, too. I feared he would become emotionally unstable and have what is widely termed a "nervous breakdown." The genuine efforts

God's Talk

I made to understand the severe conflicts between us were largely unsuccessful.

While the real estate market was good, we decided to sell the Crystal Lake property and hopefully lower the stress levels we were dealing with. It wasn't easy to give up our comfortable home in the spacious country setting, but it was way too much work. We were pleased, though, with the financial outcome of the sale, and we learned some valuable lessons along the way. We moved back to our house that we had rented out to Wycliffe members.

Resignation from WBT - September 1981

A result of this time of turmoil was that Carl became involved in conduct that was contrary to Biblical principles as well as to Wycliffe policy and was unfaithful in his marriage commitment. As a result, he was required to resign from the organization.

Carl writes:

> I was asked to abruptly resign from Wycliffe. Marilyn filed for divorce. She decided that she must bow out of the picture, having done her best to be a faithful, supportive wife.

Marilyn faces unexpected changes:

> My greatest desire was to continue with Wycliffe as a full member even though we were divorced. The policy at that time, however, stated that a member who initiated a divorce could not remain a member, even though he/she was not at fault. The

Work at the International Linguistic Center in Dallas, Texas

Wycliffe Board of Directors denied my request to remain a full member. It was a very difficult choice to have to face.

While living separately, Carl and I had long, late night telephone conversations. Within a few weeks Carl reported that he was confronting his weaknesses and felt strong enough to resist temptation. He began to pressure me to not go through with the divorce, assuring me that he would commit himself anew to our marriage.

I had taken my marriage vows seriously, "for better, for worse, for richer or poorer, in sickness and in health." I decided to listen to my conscience and give him the benefit of the doubt. I dropped the divorce proceedings.*

At that time, the WBT protocol was that a married couple had to both be members. Since Carl had been asked to leave, that meant I had to resign as well. So with painful reluctance and deep, exquisite sadness, I submitted my resignation to Wycliffe. Leaving the work that I loved was a very traumatic experience. Grieving this loss hurt worse than the prospect of a divorce!

*A more complete picture of our journey can be found in our book, "*The "Ideal" Couple: The Shadow Side of a Marriage*" available through Amazon.com, Barnes & Noble, and Cascadia Publishing House.

God's Talk

A Brief Summary of the Years 1982-1996

Resignation from the mission meant we needed to notify our faithful financial supporters that we were no longer Wycliffe members so their support could go toward others. Now another phase of our lives began. We bought a home in Garland, a suburb of Dallas, and worked in secular jobs the next six years--Carl at typesetting and I as a mental health nurse in two hospitals, Richardson and Garland.

God Calls A New Team

In the summer of 1984, Chris and Elaine Hurst informed us they felt God calling them to take up the work among the Aztecs. What an answer to our prayers for someone to replace us! We were thrilled that the work would continue. The next eight weeks we helped them learn all they could about the Nahuatl language before they set out for Mexico. They chose to settle in Tatahuicapan, a larger town than Mecayapan. Adjusting to life there with their two young children had some stiff challenges. The townspeople accepted them, and it wasn't long until they were deep into Nahuatl language study and establishing friendships with the Aztec people.

The Hursts distributed the books of the Nahuatl Grammar that had been published shortly before. They were eagerly received by the Mexican government and the schools in the Aztec towns. It was also a big boost to the prestige of the Nahuatl language. The people were beginning to take pride in their heart-language by then. They could see that it had a definite structure just like other languages. So it wasn't gibberish after all.

In August 1987 I accepted a position on the nursing staff of Prairie View Mental Health Center in Newton, Kansas. We sold our house in Garland and moved to an apartment in Newton. Carl worked at a typesetting shop in Wichita, but a year later was laid off after desk-top publishing took over. He decided to enroll in a Master's degree program at Wichita State University.

Then, in 1989 came distressing news when he was diagnosed with early stages of Parkinson's disease. We both depended on daily strength from God, along with more counseling. Carl graduated with honors from Wichita State in May 1994. He taught for two years until he retired in May 1996. I also retired from Prairie View after almost ten years.

The Bilingual Dictionary Project: 1996 - 2002

Now that we were retired, what were we going to do that was productive and satisfying? We took a bold step by telling Chris and Elaine we were willing to help them with the language work in any way they saw possible. They immedi-

A Brief Summary of the Years 1982-1996

ately suggested we compile the bilingual Nahuatl-Spanish dictionary that we started years before, using the stacks of language data that all of us had collected over the years. Elaine laboriously keyboarded an estimated 5,000 words and their meanings on the computer, ready for us to sift through and choose which ones to include. Gladly we accepted and tackled this challenge. We knew it would be an awesome, almost intimidating task but one that we knew would eventually promote use of the Scriptures in Nahuatl and give additional prestige to the body of literature already produced.

We bought our first computer with internet capabilities and took up the Nahuatl language work again with renewed zeal. It was fascinating to communicate across all those miles by e-mail with the Hursts and their two native language associates, Placido and Esteban, in Mexico. We were novices at making dictionaries, so to help us get started, we attended two six-week workshops in Mexico that were specially designed for compiling bilingual dictionaries. The first one was in November 1996, and second one was held in January 1998. Expert advice was available on how to format a dictionary in two languages. Working with Placido, Esteban and Chris was a tremendously exciting experience. During the next four years of working on our own, we spent many tedious hours at our computer, using a special program for formatting bilingual dictionaries.

In May 2001 we drove to the Mexico Branch Center in Tucson, Arizona where we consulted with linguistic experts on some of the final details. In August 2002, we submitted the dictionary manuscript for publication. It was printed in 2003 and was welcomed with great enthusiasm in the Nahuatl language areas and in government circles--another example of how Nahuatl was steadily gaining acceptance in high places. Both the grammar and dictionary can be accessed on

God's Talk

the Internet at this location: www.sil.org/americas/mexico.

We look forward to the time when the Isthmus New Testament is completed and available to the people. We are happy to note that progress steadily continues through the dedicated help of capable and enthusiastic Aztec Christians! Chris and Elaine have faithfully directed the work we began. Three loyal Christian Aztec men, Placido, Esteban and Hilario, have worked steadily with Hursts on translation and literacy through the years. Currently all three of the Aztec co-workers are happily involved in a growing evangelism and literacy program among their own people in the Nahuatl language. There were many others, too numerous to mention here, including the pastors of growing congregations, who had a hand in teaching us the language, diligently worked with us on Scripture translation, literacy, the grammar, and the dictionary. We pray that they continue to minister to their own people.

It is deeply gratifying to hear reports of new converts and congregations springing up in that area. Native pastors in at least fifteen congregations are now using the Scriptures in the services. Under Chris's direction, several pastors formed a "translation committee" to assure accuracy of the final manuscripts.

The people are excited about their ability to read the Scriptures. They sing native-authored songs, preach and pray in their very own heart language. We expect to be joined by our Aztec friends and thousands of other language groups as we sing praises to God around the Throne. The apostle John wrote in Revelation 7:9-10: *After these things, I looked and behold, a great multitude, which no one could count, from every nation and all tribes, peoples and tongues, standing before the throne and before the Lamb, clothed in white robes with palm branches in their hands saying ..."Salvation to our God who sits on the throne and to the Lamb!" (The American Standard Version)*

It is important here that we again acknowledge the devoted efforts of Dr. Howard and Joan Law, the first Wycliffe translators who paved the way in the early fifties by nurturing friendships and producing preliminary literature for the Isthmus Aztec people. Through their witness and initial attempts at Scripture translation, several Aztec people became believers and began meeting together. These dear Christians multiplied and were still meeting together when we arrived a few years later.

A Special Honor: Alumni Christian Service Award

Awesome news came to us in July 2004. We were literally speechless when the Alumni Director of Messiah College, our alma mater, informed us that we had been chosen to receive the Alumni Christian Service Award for Outstanding Christian Service. Our first reaction was shock and awe--a sense of being totally unworthy of such a commendation.

We reflected on how God's power and promises have sustained us in the face of seemingly insurmountable difficulties. His purposes are often accomplished through imperfect people. Even with all our weaknesses, vulnerabilities and handicaps, He will accomplish His purpose for our lives and further His Kingdom.

Memories of the emotional stress we experienced are reminders to praise God for His sustaining grace. We rejoice that He has called and equipped others to step in to fill the gap. All this is in God's hands, and we trust in His perfect timing. It has been rewarding and fulfilling to have had a part in carrying out His Great Commission--to share the Gospel with the Aztecs by providing the written Word in their own heart language.

In October of 2004 we gratefully accepted the Christian Service Award to honor our work in Bible Translation, linguistic analysis, literacy, community service and medical work among the Aztec people in a lovely ceremony that took place at the Messiah College alumni banquet. On this occasion, it was especially heart-warming to personally acknowledge several of our fellow-alumni who had supported us with letters, prayers and finances through the years. We owe even more people a huge debt of gratitude. The attractive award plaque is inscribed this way:

**The Alumni Association of Messiah College,
Grantham, Pennsylvania,
presents to J. Carl and Marilyn J. Wolgemuth
the Alumni Christian Service Award
for Outstanding Christian Service**

**"This award recognizes outstanding long-term effort
in fulfilling the mandates of the Christian gospel
to both serve and sacrifice for the needs of humanity."**

*signed, Kim Phipps, PhD, President;
Randall Ness, Director of Alumni Relations*

Acknowledgments

There are a multitude of people who we would like to mention that have had a profound effect on our lives down through the years. To name them all would be a book in itself.

We begin with early childhood influences that sparked our interest in reaching out to others--our parents and Sunday School teachers. We were captivated and intrigued by reading books about missions and the dangers that go with treading in uncharted territory. Returning missionaries impressed us with their courage, like David and Mabel Hall who reported their harrowing experiences on their way to Africa during WW II. As they crossed the Atlantic with their two small children on the Egyptian ship ZamZam, a German warship torpedoed the ship and sank it. The passengers barely escaped with their lives.

During college days, peers and professors reinforced our desire to someday be actively involved in missions. President C.N. Hostetter, Prof. Albert Engle, Professors Charles and

God's Talk

Mary Eshelman, who had served many years in Africa, were among the many others who modeled a selfless commitment to Christian Service.

Our heartfelt thanks goes to the many prayer partners and financial donors--too numerous to mention each by name, but that know who you are--who responded to Godly nudges and stood by us during the twenty years we were members of Wycliffe. Without their support, we would have been unable to stay on task.

Some of our dearest friends and mentors were Wycliffe colleagues who encouraged us through the rougher times: Walt and Marilyn Agee, Frank and Ethel Robbins, Ted and Trish Goller, Bob and Carol Chaney, Ralph and Marey Todd, Al and Delores Rice, Cal and Carolyn Rensch, John and Jean Alsop.

Chris and Elaine Hurst, to whom we "passed the torch," continue to steadily work with Aztec pastors and lay Christians to complete the translation of the Isthmus Nahuatl New Testament, Old Testament Stories and other literature.

We anticipate Dedication Day when it will be available to all who speak the Isthmus Nahuatl language.

Three extraordinary Nahuatl speakers, who have worked closely with the Hursts and us over many years, must be given special mention: Esteban Ramirez, Placido Hernandez and Hilario Salas. These three men are totally committed to and enthusiastic about having the Scriptures in their own language and teaching their own people.

Acknowledgments

Our pastor at First Presbyterian Church in Duncanville, Rev. John C. Poling and his dear wife, Jackie, were so helpful when we needed them at a crucial time. We made close friends at that church also with C. A. and Joyce Buster, J. and Wanda Rubrecht and Betty Murphy to name a few.

On our frequent peregrinations to and from Mexico we appreciated family connections: Aunt Bonnie Luker in Oklahoma City always welcomed us with a refreshing stop-over. Our cousins, Ernest and Betty Frey, Jack and Shirley Frey, Dick and Shirley Ann Frey lovingly provided wonderful southern hospitality and family fun times in the Houston, Texas area. Also in Houston, Dr. Buddy Gregory, DDS offered to care for our dental needs when we came through. He donated his time and resources so generously to provide the three of us with state-of-the-art dental care. What a gift!

In order to portray Wycliffe Bible Translators and the Summer Institute of Linguistics in the most accurate way, we asked two Wycliffe editors, colleagues Mae Toedter and Kathy Lehardy, to go over the manuscript. They carefully edited the contents and smoothed out several passages. We very much appreciate their gracious gift of time and energy. Thank you, Mae and Kathy.

And last but far from least, we give thanks to our daughter Carrie who shared the village life and work with us for fourteen years. She is now giving her time and energy to publish this memoir for us--a gift for which we express our deepest gratitude.

God's Talk

Acknowledgments

CPSIA information can be obtained at www.ICGtesting.com
Printed in the USA
LVOW031535151111
255104LV00002B/70/P